A BLUEPRINT FOR BUILDING CHILDREN: FOLLOWING GOD'S PLAN

Stephanie DeGen  M.S. Ed.

RAIN PUBLISHING

Duluth, GA

A Blueprint for Building Children: Following God's Plan
by Stephanie Modesta DeGeneste, M.S. Ed.
Contact: stephanie@wgcdproductions.com
Rain Publishing
www.RainPublishing.com

Original cover art by Kyle Olani Adams www.betherenaissance.com

Cover design by www.7streamsmedia.com.

Unless otherwise noted, Scriptures are taken from the HOLY BIBLE, New King James Version

Scriptures noted NIV are taken from the New International Version of the Bible.
Scriptures noted AMP are taken from the Amplified Bible.
Scriptures noted LB are taken from the Living Bible translation of the Bible.
Scriptures noted ESV are taken from the English Standard Version of the Bible.
Scriptures noted CEV are taken from the Contemporary English Version of the Bible.
Scriptures noted CEB are taken from the Contemporary English Bible.
Scriptures noted NET are taken from the New English Translation Bible.
Scriptures noted KJV are taken from the King James Version Bible.
Scriptures noted NRSV are taken from the New Revised Standard Version Bible.
Scriptures noted NLT are taken from the New Living Translation Bible.

A Blueprint for Building Children: Following God's Plan. First Edition
Stephanie Modesta DeGeneste, M.S. Ed.
ISBN: 979-8-9927864-4-6

Library of Congress Control Number: 2025926405

A Blueprint For Building Children: Following God's Plan is dedicated to my precious parents, Charles Edward and Barbara Theresa Smith. They are God's special gift to me. Whether on this plane of earthly existence or in the realms of glory, their presence in my life is the gift that keeps on giving. Their limitless, unconditional, and always supportive love paved the way for me to thrive in my endeavors. Even when I made mistakes, and there were many along the way, they were among the loudest voices in the cheering section, encouraging me to learn something valuable and move on. How great is my love and appreciation for them.

Readers from three generations provide reflections about
A Blueprint For Building Children: Following God's Plan

A Blueprint For Building Children: Following God's Plan is an essential read for Christian parents aiming to infuse their parenting with Christian values. The author masterfully blends profound theological insights with practical guidance, presenting a fresh perspective on nurturing a child's spiritual and emotional development. Each chapter offers actionable advice, real-life anecdotes, and reflective insights, making it easier to navigate the complexities of parenting. ~Dr. Erika Richardson, Wife, Mother Of Two, Professor

A Blueprint For Building Children: Following God's Plan aligns with God's Word and Stephanie's heart. Blueprint is not a theoretical dive into parenting; it's a Biblical road map supported by Scripture and verse detailing how God desires us to parent HIS children. If you love your children, if you want to honor God, then adhere to God's plan for them. Blueprint is an easy-to-follow, thorough approach to parenting that guides while on the path of excellence God's way. It confirms that God's way is timeless; it stands throughout generations. ~Nadine E. Medley, Active Grandparent, Sister In The Faith And In The Trenches

A Blueprint For Building Children: Following God's Plan is such a refreshing read as a mother currently walking through toddlerhood. Stephanie is so intentional with how she incorporates Biblical parenting with real-life scenarios. I feel seen while being convicted and educated at the same time. She uses Scripture to back up her material with practical applications that are thoughtfully laid out for the reader. This book is such a blessing for parents who truly want to raise their children with a Biblical foundation. ~Sarah Atkins, Wife, Mother, Early Childhood Educator.

CONTENTS

Introduction

Before making a simple margin note in my well-worn Bible, I asked myself more than a few times, "Why should I write a book about raising children?" I also asked myself two specific questions: 1. So, what do you think you can contribute to the vast body of material related to raising children that doesn't already exist? and 2. Will people even bother to read something about raising children that is not written by one of the renowned experts who has already published numerous books on the subject? Of course, a few other questions came to mind, but I think you get the drift. I prayed for several weeks after a very persuasive life coach started urging me to write this type of book. Subsequently, several people whom I hold in high regard were jumping on the bandwagon as well. Finally, I wrote the following margin note to God, "To God be the glory. I dedicate Blueprint the book to You, dear Lord. 11/26/14." When I read Psalm 45:1 that early November morning, the prompting was so strong that I made a vow to the Lord - and I am one who deems vows to God very important and binding. That verse states, "My heart is overflowing with a good theme; I recite my composition concerning the King; My tongue is the pen of a ready writer." Truly, my heart is overflowing with a good theme when it comes to lavishing praise and honor on my King, who I sincerely believe is the best source of help when it comes to seeking out the most advantageous way to raise children.

To be perfectly candid, though my heart continued to be overflowing with a good theme, many obstacles got in the way, and I grew discouraged because I wasn't making significant progress writing *A Blueprint For Building Children: Following God's Plan*. As the years passed by, on more than one occasion, I thought about not completing the project. But again and again, my heart was stirred by the Word of God. Psalm 56:12 and 13 state, "Vows made to You are binding upon me, O God; I will render praises to You, for You have delivered my soul from death. Have You not kept my feet from falling, that I may walk before God in the light of the living?" As I prayed for the fortitude and faithfulness needed to complete this book, I felt that if only one family profited from anything written on its pages, then that was reason enough to complete *A Blueprint For Building Children: Following God's Plan.* There were countless times in the parenting process when God kept my feet from falling. Oh, how I pray God will strengthen and equip you to face the challenges associated with parenting, as He faithfully helped me through the years.

Among the definitions found in The American Heritage Dictionary, a blueprint is a detailed plan of action, a model, or a prototype.[1] We see several places in the Word of God where Jesus expresses His high regard for children, and Psalm 127:3 in the New Living Translation states, "Children are a gift from the Lord; they are a reward from him." The Lord has given children to us as gifts to be treasured. That is an important fact to ponder. There shouldn't be any doubt in our minds that when something is important to God, He'll provide the divine direction; yes, I daresay the blueprint and all the resources we need to achieve the outstanding outcomes He has in mind for our children, the precious gifts entrusted to us.

I am well aware of what God can do when Biblical principles are the sure foundation upon which you build your parenting process. I have the distinct privilege of having a biological daughter and son who were born twenty years and three months to the day from one another. I also have a bonus daughter (I gave up the typical term stepdaughter years ago) who is one year older than my biological daughter. What that means is, for all intents and purposes, I have raised my beloved children through two different generations. Why is that important? Though trends and technology may change, God's Word does not change. I have seen over and over again that God's Word prevails over all things; it withstands the test of time just as it is written in Isaiah 40:8, "The grass withers, the flower fades, but the word of our God stands forever." The Bible is eternal truth, and it remains relevant and profitable in our challenging times. Consider what is stated in 2 Timothy 3:15-17 in the Living Bible translation, "The whole Bible was given to us by inspiration from God and is useful to teach us what is true and to make us realize what is wrong in our lives; it straightens us out and helps us do what is right. It is God's way of making us prepared at every point, fully equipped to do good to everyone."

I have seen and experienced so many things firsthand during the last fifty years as I have raised my own children and worked with thousands of children in my role as a career educator. Sad to say, what compelled me to develop an interactive workshop entitled *A Blueprint For Building Children: Following God's Plan* still stirs my heart because, if anything, the plight of children nowadays is far worse than three decades ago. Youth problems abound: low academic performance, tobacco, alcohol, and drug use, premarital sex leading to far too many cases of sexually transmitted diseases or premature motherhood and fatherhood, child abuse, gang activity, bullying, suicide, homicide, and the list goes on. The reality is this: children mirror the behavior of the adults who are responsible for their care. Countless adults today are raising children by default and not by design. And what is the result? Over and over again...DISASTER. In the New International Version in Jeremiah 29:11, we see, "'For I know the plans I have for you,' declares the Lord, 'plans to prosper you and not to harm you, plans to give you hope and a future.'" Clearly, God's plan for His children is for good. God is infinitely wiser than we are, and He has an impeccable track record that is being ignored en masse by today's Christians. Again, I ask, what is the result? Far too often, devastating unintended consequences are cascading down upon our families and pummeling us like unleashed floodwaters careening onto land when the levee breaks.

There has been a disturbing trend to veer away from the wisdom of the Bible in favor of following man's notions of what is best. I suppose what I hope this book will accomplish is to sound a clarion call that it's time to take the parable of the builders to heart. Adults who are responsible for the care of children can either build on the rock-solid foundation of God's word or the ever-shifting sands of trendy ideas. In both Matthew 7:24-27 and Luke 6:47-49, Jesus clearly states that everyone who hears His sayings and does not do them will be like a foolish man who built his house on the sand: and the rain descended, the floods came, and the wind blew and beat upon that house, and it fell, and great was its fall. The storms of life will assail every person's existence, but the outcomes will vary based on the foundational underpinnings that support an individual's decision-making in the midst of adversities.

My deepest desire is to provide a book about raising children that is steeped in Scripture and one that contains practical suggestions you can implement in your daily life. *Soli Deo Gloria* is the Latin expression Glory to God alone. This book is offered to you with the glory of God and the building up of children, God's gift to us, in the forefront of my mind. With every fiber of my being, I want to encourage you to let the Bible be your guide as you raise and care for children. You'll be overjoyed by the results.

ONE

The Divine Pattern for the Family

Today's family demographics span the gamut as it relates to the age of parents and a myriad of other factors like marital status, level of formal education earned, occupations, socioeconomic status, sexual orientation, cultural influences, parenting styles, etc. Of course, every family is unique, joined together by its own array of particular circumstances. Unique families have been the case for time immemorial; nevertheless, it seems the sheer number of variations related to today's family units have eclipsed previous generations, and because that is the case, there seem to be more questions, ambiguities, challenges, and frustrations related to the parenting process than ever before.

Prior to the 1950s, family structures were not nearly as diverse as they are now. Traditional two-parent homes were the norm, and typically, the mother stayed home to care for the children. Here are some of the family units and situations that exist today:

- Two-parent households with any of the following configurations: both parents work, and the children are cared for by an outside extended-care program or a live-in helper; either one of the parents is the stay-at-home caregiver, or another relative cares for the children.
- Two-parent households where children are cared for by a disabled or temporarily unemployed parent.

- Single-parent households where children are cared for by an extended-care program outside the home or a live-in helper, or a relative or other trusted adult cares for the children outside the home as the parent goes out to work.
- Adoptive parents in any of the aforementioned scenarios.
- The "ready-made" family is where one or both parents enter the marriage with children from a previous relationship or as a result of a family-related crisis.
- Foster parents with varying situations.

Accompanying the matter of whether one or two parents reside in the home, along with the possibility of other extended family members living in the home permanently or temporarily, the fact that a temporary situation may exist, such as:

- One or both parents are away on a military deployment assignment.
- One or both parents are incarcerated.
- One or both parents are on business assignments that require extended time away from home.
- One or both parents are unemployed.

Still, another factor that is evident today is families where parents are:

- LGBTQ+, which according to Dictionary.com, pertains collectively to people who identify as lesbian, gay, bisexual, or transgender, and to people with gender expressions outside traditional norms, including nonbinary, intersex, and other queer people (and those questioning their gender identity or sexual orientation), along with their allies.[1]

Why are any of the previously mentioned parenting configurations germane to the discussion at hand? Do any or all of these factors play into how children are raised today? Children are not raised in a vacuum, and familial situations always come with challenges. Parental choices have consequences.

The complexities of parenting, definitely a demanding and difficult job in any situation, truly increase as more and more variables factor into the mix. This chapter seeks to present the divine pattern for the family not as a means of oversimplification but to indicate certain priorities from a Biblical point of view. Perhaps what is said will represent relatively new concepts for certain readers and provide some food for thought.

Human beings are made in the image of God and patterned after His nature (Genesis 1:27). Parenting's origin story was authored by the Lord Himself, so clearly, the family is near and dear to God's heart. If we look in the very first book of the Bible, Genesis, we don't see the church, some vocational enterprise, or a form of government established first; no, we see God creating Eve, so Adam wouldn't have to be alone, and then, without skipping a beat, the Lord states, "Be fruitful and multiply." Adam says of Eve in Genesis 2:23, "This is now bone of my bones and flesh of my flesh, she shall be called Woman, because she was taken out of Man." Genesis 2:24 provides the words still used in some marriage ceremonies today, "Therefore a man shall leave his father and mother and be joined to his wife, and they shall become one flesh." I don't know about you, but I find it really interesting that the marital relationship was established as the first human institution. Everyone can clearly see the diversity and suitability of the male and female bodies to facilitate procreation. The wonderful union of marriage, originated by God, provided the proper context for children to follow as a means of securing the family lineage and providing posterity for the parents. The divine order, married parents first and children second, helps to foster stability and security for little ones.

In the New Testament book of Ephesians in 5:22-6:4, the Apostle Paul expounds on marital roles in relation to how the husband and wife should relate to Christ and to one another, as well as how the children are to relate to their parents. While many find the words submission and obedience archaic as it relates to relationships, when one studies the principles that are espoused in the aforementioned passage, looking through a lens of humble submission and God-honoring obedience, a different perspective comes into view. God's intent is never to harm us but to provide for us and protect us from so many unintended consequences that come into our lives due to foolish choices, choices made simply because we do not possess sufficient understanding, or we choose to ignore God's infinite wisdom.

A marital relationship should never be entered into unadvisedly. It is a state of being that should not be taken lightly. Successful marriages produce stability, and stable homes produce secure, happy children. From a Biblical perspective, the following greatly increase the probability of a successful marriage: salvation, faithful church attendance, personal Bible study, prayer, regular family devotions, and serving the Lord together.

No doubt, the wheels of some readers' minds may be turning or hearts churning depending on what someone focuses on. Let me be perfectly transparent: I remember being so upset about certain marital principles found in Scripture upon my first encounters with the information. I engaged in pre-marital sex when I was 18. I married my first husband at age 20 and had my daughter at age 23. I was divorced by the age of 26 and remarried by the age of 30, all before I had any clue about the divine pattern for the family. I also engaged in sexual activity prior to my second marriage, an activity that still evokes a measure of remorse to this day. Given my present age (over 70) and stage of life, I can look back on my experiences and see where different choices would have provided much better outcomes, but truth be told, I was ignorant and rebellious about so many things. I don't think it was until I fully embraced Jeremiah 29:11 that bears repeating, in which God states, "For I know the thoughts that I think toward you, says the Lord, thoughts of peace and not of evil, to give you a future and a hope," that I stopped fighting God tooth and nail about everything. It was time to stop doubting that His ways would make an appreciable difference in my life. God's ways will make an appreciable difference in any life, as He is no respecter of persons. What He's done for me and my family, He can do for you.

Firm family foundations are built on the cornerstone of Christ. This book is entitled *A Blueprint For Building Children: Following God's Plan* because the Lord is an awesome architect, and His plans for us are good. We have to be cognizant of His plans and be willing to follow Him as He leads us in the execution of the plan. Believe me, I know that it is so very hard to do. Nevertheless, no matter how difficult the journey, the untold blessings we derive along the way are well worth it.

I'd like to share a word about divorce, remarriage, and single parenting before the close of this chapter. Simply put, we see in Malachi 2:16 that God hates divorce. The Lord desires that marriages be permanent. Extensive premarital counseling with a qualified professional that touches on the typical flashpoints in a marriage should occur unhurriedly, preferably over the course of a year or more, before the vows are recited. Couples spend thousands and thousands of dollars and countless hours planning elaborate weddings, yet some refuse to spend a few hundred dollars and devote a designated number of hours to engage in premarital and/or marital counseling.

Divorce and remarriage create a new set of issues and, far too frequently, specific problems that open the family up for turmoil that God never intended. Blended families are far more complex to navigate than intact first-marriage families. I speak from experience in that both my husband and I brought along a daughter born during our previous marriages when we married in 1980. We didn't have any premarital counseling before we stepped into marriage number two. So, not only do I have personal lived experience in this area, but I also have observed countless second and third-marriage interactions in my role as a career educator. I have seen quite a bit of drama in blended families during my 50+ years of teaching experience. Typically, blended families are conceived as a result of some sort of loss: the death of a spouse or the deathblows that destroyed one or two previous marriages. Make no mistake about it: one or more children coming into a new family situation because of remarriage can be scarred. The wounds are often very deep. While it is bad enough that hurt abounds, ambiguity is also rampant. These two factors typically impact blended families in virtually every facet of family living as they pertain to interactions with biological and stepparents and grandparents. This is especially the case when the key people involved are ill-prepared for the realities that they'll be facing. That certainly was the case in my situation. Our girls were five and six years old when they met and seven and eight years old when we married. Without premarital counseling, my husband and I were clueless, and by the two-year mark, our marriage was in the throes of crisis. We were on the fast track to divorce number two. I gave my life to Christ in the midst of the madness, and I know without the grace of God and the help of godly people in the form of their prayers and sound advice, our marriage would have tragically ended before year three. It's no surprise to me that the complexities inherent in second marriages result in a 60-67% failure rate, according to Reference.com, thus re-traumatizing children who are involved in these broken relationships. Please do not think I'm advocating that people stay in abusive relationships just for the sake of their children. That is brutally detrimental for abused individuals. I do, however, believe that no stone should be left unturned when it comes to employing specific strategies to preserve and fortify existing marriages.

Single parenting can be very temporary, short-term, or longer-term. It results from various situations, among them: hospitalization, extended business or military assignments, incarceration, abandonment, divorce or separation, fornication, adultery, rape, or death of a spouse, to name a few. Single parenting represents parenting stresses and strains on steroids. The daily struggles are real, and single parents must cultivate support systems to help with their ongoing challenges. This is where membership in a non-judgmental local church or an affiliation with a supportive family-oriented organization can be the balm of Gilead to help heal wounds. So many of the aforementioned situations do not represent God's ideal. Any one predicament can result in an array of taxing problems to deal with. Yet, the Lord is faithful to provide the grace and any other needed resources to care for children, His beloved heritage.

If you are in a challenging situation, take steps to stabilize your condition. Don't let sin destroy your home. Squarely face the events that led to your present scenario. Confess whatever sin is involved and beg God's forgiveness. He will forgive you and cleanse you from all unrighteousness (1 John 1:19).

Not only should you confess your sins, but you should strive to resolve differences with key people (i.e., former partners, parents, children, etc.). Seek help from the Body of Christ. Seek help from professional Christian counselors. Free yourself from pride, guilt, anger, fear, and shame, as all these emotions block God's blessings. Commit to doing things God's way, not man's way, from now on. Move forward in His strength and enabling power. God is not the author of confusion. He has established a divine pattern for the family. As we submit to God and to one another in our relationships, the Lord will bring about His divine outcomes for our family.

TWO

Children Learn What They Live

From the first time I saw a poster-size version of Dorothy Nolte's poem, "Children Learn What They Live," I was struck by the simple but profound truths that are presented for the reader or listener to ponder. When I conduct the interactive parenting workshop that bears the same name as this book, I try to have a young child recite the poem that follows. Imagine, if you will, the sweet, precious sound of a high-pitched voice so eager to please the one who made the request, the little voice that captivates every adult listener as she or he says:

"Children Learn What They Live" by Dorothy Nolte

If a child lives with criticism, He learns to condemn.
If a child lives with hostility, He learns to fight.
If a child lives with ridicule, He learns to be shy.
If a child lives with shame, He learns to feel guilty.
If a child lives with tolerance, He learns to be patient.
If a child lives with encouragement, He learns confidence.
If a child lives with praise, He learns to appreciate.
If a child lives with fairness, He learns justice.
If a child lives with security, He learns to have faith.
If a child lives with approval, He learns to like himself.

If a child lives with acceptance and friendship, He learns to find love in the world.

Children, especially very young children, are like sponges; they soak up whatever is around them, be it good, bad, indifferent, toxic, or terrific. It's rather amazing how their voices copy the same vocal inflections when they're saying something that Mommy or Daddy would say, oftentimes to the parents' great chagrin. And then there are the children who even master their parents' gestures and facial expressions. Let's face it, children's personalities, attitudes, reactions, and desires largely mirror those of their parents or primary caregivers. When you look at the children in your care, what are they reflecting?

Children learn to walk, talk, eat, etc. by example. What type of example are you setting for your own children and the children who come into contact with you on a regular basis? Parents or other adult caregivers who have problems with hostility, profanity, bitterness, or lack of forgiveness, immorality, laziness, pride, arrogance, or other negative character traits often see the same patterns of behavior repeated in their children. How you live is crucial! When parents are living joyful, successful Christian lives representing the character of Christ, it is far easier to train their children to follow in their footsteps.

In 1 Peter 2:21, we see, "For to this you were called, because Christ also suffered for us, leaving us an example, that you should follow His steps." Christ is our paradigm of virtue. He is the perfect role model for us, and as we follow in His footsteps, we lead lives that make it evident to our own children and any other children that we may be able to influence, that our pattern of behavior will not lead them down the wrong path. A God-centered life helps us stay in the circle of God's perfect will for our lives. John Stormer presents the following seven prerequisites for a God-centered life in his book *Growing Up God's Way*.[1]

1. Know God personally
2. Obey Him
3. Be thankful for everything
4. Be honest with yourself, with God, and with others
5. Resolve all differences with others God's way
6. Know and accept God's purpose for your life and learn what He has done to fulfill His purpose in you
7. Live for others rather than yourself

Are you currently living a God-centered life? Assess where you are at this point in time, and as number 4 states, be honest with yourself. Even if you're not at all happy with your honest assessment, try not to be discouraged. One of my favorite quotes is by educator and civil rights activist, Dr. Mary McLeod Bethune. I encountered her sage words as I read her life story. She said, "Neither God nor man can use a discouraged soul." You can be encouraged as you parent your children because if Christ is your personal Savior, the words of 2 Corinthians 5:17 can resonate in your heart and provide the impetus to make requisite changes in your life. That passage of Scripture states, "Therefore if anyone is in Christ, he isa new creation: old things have passed away; behold, all things have become new." If you're not sure that Christ is your Savior, then you can turn to Appendix A in this book and read what the Simple Plan of Salvation entails and make a concrete decision about that today.

In keeping with honest introspection, take some time to be brutally frank with yourself. Get out a piece of paper, draw a line down the center of it, and put the following heading on the paper: Positive Influences/Negative Influences. Don't stop writing until you exhaust your mind of all the things that you do on a regular basis that are both positive and negative. If you're really courageous, you can ask your spouse, partner, older children, or a trusted friend to give you some input. Do you think they don't notice how you routinely raise your voice in anger or frustration, habitually drive over the speed limit, or lie when you don't want to speak to a particular person on the phone? Of course, they do! On the flip side of the coin, you may not think that the love notes you tuck into lunch bags are a big deal or that showing up to games is that important. You'll want these things to make it to your list. You'd be surprised how getting additional input can add to your entries. Hopefully, related to your life, there are a lot more positive influences than negative ones. I'm sure that will be the case. At this point, you should endeavor to look at yourself in a balanced, honest way.

Since you should not ignore the fact that children learn what they live, it's important for you to live in a God-honoring way to help educate your children effectively. "Education... is a painful and difficult work to be done in kindness, by watching, by warning, ...by praise, but above all–by example." ~ John Ruskin.[2] Also consider the quote that follows, which is another favorite of mine: "Home is the first classroom, and parents are the first teachers." ~ Unknown. Parent, you are a teacher, whether you think so or not, whether you fully embrace that particular role or not. And whether or not you recognize you're teaching your children something day in and day out, that is what is happening. I'd like to underscore that with a brief anecdote. My son was quite young when he received Christ as his Savior. The church he grew up in had a very solid youth ministry, and I knew he was learning Bible truths at church and at home, but what I really didn't understand sufficiently was the power of my role modeling until a particular incident. It was the first time my son was going to receive communion. Leading up to that moment, I had reviewed the significance of the Lord's Table with him, and I knew he had learned about it at Sunday School, but I was still a little anxious as the elements were being passed out that he might immediately start eating the bread and not wait for the instructions from the pastor. Or perhaps he'd be careless with the juice and spill it all over the place, so I leaned over to mention what he should be doing, and he said with confidence, "Oh, I know what to do; I have been watching you." That statement had a profound impact on me.

Your child usually gets a new teacher or group of teachers every year, but he or she interacts with you day after day, month after month, year after year. What are your children learning from you? Keep in mind that your children are the messages you send to a time you will never see. What future messages will your children deliver to the world around them? Will their actions speak loudly that it's okay to lie, cheat, steal, gossip, malign someone's character, intimidate, discriminate, or hate? For the love of God, you should emphatically be saying, "NO!" I'm sure you've heard the expression, "The apple doesn't fall far from the tree." Psalm 1 depicts the type of tree you should endeavor to be. When you delight yourself in the law of the Lord and meditate on it day and night, you shall be like a tree planted by the rivers of water that brings forth its fruit in its season. It's likely your children are already the apple of your eye. Make a commitment today that they will not become rotten apples but the type of luscious fruit that anyone who encounters your children will be able to taste and see that the Lord is good.

Now, go back to your list of positive and negative influences. Zero in on one of the negative influences. Circle or place an asterisk by that particular trait. Take a moment to write a brief prayer asking God's help to correct this problem. You don't need a lot of words or fancy words when you pray. Just tell God how you feel and ask for help. You can say something as simple as, "Lord, I know I have a bad temper, and I'm really hurting my children when I lash out at them. These days, I seem to be angry all the time. Many times, I'm out of control. Please help me do what I need to do to correct the problem." The Lord hears your sincere cries for assistance. The awesome thing about God is that He will send help your way. Now, don't get persnickety about where the help comes from or make a bunch of excuses, give lots of pushback on the matter, or keep procrastinating. If someone gives you an anger management book, don't use the book as a coaster for your favorite beverage; get busy and read it. Perhaps at some point along the way, you have received some feedback from your pastor, a good friend, or your spouse that seeing a Christian counselor would be beneficial. Try not to be offended.

Believe that person has your best interests and your children's best interests at heart. Going to a Christian counselor and, as time passed, obtaining a Christian Counseling Diploma from the Christian Counseling & Educational Foundation in Laverock, PA, was very helpful to me and made a significant impact on the way I approached parenting.

The list of positive and negative influences you delineated should not be placed under a pile of papers or tucked away in a desk drawer. Keep it visible or readily available. Perhaps a good place for your list would be on your phone, on a bulletin board, or anywhere that's in plain sight. Remember, out of sight...out of mind. Be sure to augment and enhance the positive influences on your list.

Whittle away the negative influences over time. Just what does that mean? It means you work at maximizing your strengths and minimizing your weaknesses on a daily basis. Be devoted, diligent, and determined to improve on a daily basis. For example, if you have procrastination issues (or any other issue, for that matter), search the Internet for articles on that topic. Skim the articles for some good and workable ideas and implement them little by little, bit by bit. Another thing you can do is hook up with an accountability partner, someone you can trust to give you honest feedback and suggestions that come from a good place. These are the folks who keep us in check, but they do it so nicely because of their genuine interest in us. Know this, you won't succeed in improving every day; after all, that's unrealistic. But don't get discouraged, you'll be making steady progress if you continue to do the things that result in positive outcomes. Everyone is a work in progress. Just keep at it. You can do it! You must do it for the sake of your children's future.

Children are so special to God. We know that specifically because in Psalm 127:3, depending on the translation you reference, we see that children are a legacy from the Lord. So, you can be sure He will not fail to help you with the parenting process when it's His legacy that's ultimately on the line. Whether it's help you'll receive from reading this book or a myriad of other books on the topic, listening to a podcast, watching a parenting video, attending parenting webinars virtually, participating in person at workshops, or implementing advice from a professional counselor or some person that God sends your way, you can be certain that whatever resources you need, the Lord will bountifully supply them. God wants you to be successful in your critically important parental role. But don't ever forget that God is the Source, and everyone and everything else approved by the Lord is a resource.

Former United States Surgeon General C. Everett Koop profoundly said, "Life affords no greater responsibility, no greater privilege, than the raising of the next generation."[3] Your responsibility is to follow in Christ's footsteps so you can be the positive role model, the righteous role model your children, and, quite frankly, other people's children need you to be. Let the following quote from the May 19, 2017, *Our Daily Bread* entry soak into your soul: "Through conversation and demonstration, help prepare children to follow the Lord on the road ahead."[4] Life's roads are seldom straight and smooth; they contain plenty of curves, ruts, potholes, speed bumps, and the like to navigate. You don't want your children to be critically wounded because of a crash caused by your high-speed hypocritical behavior, do you? Children need all the help they can get for the time they must take the wheel and drive life's roads on their own. Your positive Christian testimony will be one of the most influential and compelling forces in their lives so they, too, can navigate life's roads safely and successfully. You're in a critical stage of your life journey, and you're raising and/or influencing children. Don't become distant or disengaged, distracted or dysfunctional. Keep your eye on the road and never forget for a moment that your children, and maybe more children than you'd ever imagine, are watching you and being profoundly influenced by you. As children observe your life, let it be your highest goal that they learn what godly behavior looks like and want to emulate it when they become adults. Dorothy Nolte was right on point when she said, "Children learn what they live."

THREE

Training the Whole Child

> *"I pray that God, who gives peace, will make you completely holy. And may your spirit, soul, and body be kept healthy and faultless until our Lord Jesus Christ returns."*
> *~1 Thessalonians 5:23 (CEV)*

There are three "parts" of a child's being that must be stimulated, fed, trained, and exercised:

- **Body** – consists of flesh, bones, blood, etc. Children must develop an incredible number and range of physical abilities as they move through various stages of childhood. Learning and mastering a whole array of physical skills is a painstaking, often frustrating process. Parents and other adults in children's lives must teach diligently, providing ample opportunities for them to learn new skills and giving suitable encouragement during frustrating times so they don't give in to despair when challenges or setbacks come along.
- **Soul** – consists of the mind (which thinks, reasons, and stores information), will (which decides and makes choices), and emotions (which display feelings). The soul and spirit of

children should be nurtured methodically by design rather than haphazardly by default. Parents can start forming an obedient will from infancy. Children should be challenged and trained to analyze, reason, and make sound decisions based on God's infallible Word, the Bible. Children should be taught from an early age that choices have consequences, good or bad.

- **Spirit** – consists of how one knows or senses the things of God. A parent's godly example makes a profound difference in how a child's attitudes about God and people are formed.

Each part of the child affects the function and operation of the other parts of a child's being and, consequently, her or his whole self. Some parts have greater needs at given times. For example, a sick child dictates that routines are altered, perhaps resulting in foregoing outdoor exercise, eating favorite foods, and even hearing a bedtime story and saying prayers before lights out. The doctor's orders and common sense must prevail to get through the day. Even so, body, soul, and spirit cannot be divorced from one another, though there will be times when far more emphasis is given to a particular aspect of the child's existence.

Don't neglect any part of the child's being as you focus on your child's growth and development. Day-to-day activities should be carried out deliberately to help your child reach his or her God-given potential. Nowadays, there is considerable attention paid to the physical development of children through elaborate sports programs that may be school or community sponsored. Younger and younger children are engaged in team competitions that require schedules crammed with practices and games. Many families complain that they seldom eat together, or when they do, it's a meal on the run. Homework is often done on the run, too. Sunday School teachers lament shrinking attendance on Sunday mornings due to games, sleepovers, or children so exhausted from the week's scheduling demands that they frequently miss church so they can catch up on their sleep. The atmosphere in the home is being adversely affected by the many demands or stresses and strains brought about by these outside forces. It's the wise parent that sets a God-honoring tone and tenor in the home and ensures that priorities are properly placed so that God is reverenced and not totally displaced with lesser things. Prayerful contemplation about how children are being nurtured in every facet of their being-body, soul, and spirit will help to keep order and balance in the home.

This is a perfect time to pause and take stock of the priorities that drive the decision-making around which activities your children will engage in. Priorities should be set by your family's needs, goals, and objectives, not by other family members' notions, coaches' demands, or the pressures their peers put forth. These individuals, though well-meaning, may not always have your children's needs or your family's best interests at heart. Here is a list of activities that foster family relationships, physical development, spiritual growth, and community engagement:

- Eating meals together
- Cooking and baking
- Praying
- Attending church worship services, Bible Studies, and ministry programs
- Memorizing Scripture verses and poetry
- Singing/playing musical instruments
- Contacting family members
- Gardening
- Picnicking
- Hiking
- Camping
- Reading

- Watching movies or TV programs together/ engaging in discussions about content
- Discussing current events
- Debating topics of interest and controversy
- Jogging
- Cycling
- Playing board games
- Doing puzzles
- Volunteering at church, nursing homes, soup kitchens, etc.
- Donating money to worthy causes
- Taking educational day trips
- Traveling domestically or internationally
- Learning a language together
- Playing sports together
- Attending museums, concerts, sporting events
- Helping elderly neighbors
- Writing cards and letters to missionaries, people in the military, the sick, and shut-in

As you examine the list, you'll see that some activities provide the physical exercise that growing children vitally need, while other activities stimulate the child's mind or go a long way to promote spiritual growth. What is most important is that parents do not neglect any facet of a child's well-being. Sometimes it's very straightforward what needs to be done. Just before flu season, children can get flu shots to reduce the chance of any devastating effects of the flu. When someone is sick or injured in the family, they may require medical attention, and that should not be put off. Oftentimes, today's families push past reasonable or sensible limits related to their health and well-being, resulting in unnecessary, totally avoidable consequences.

Of late, I'm shocked to see the amount of unfettered screen time little children are exposed to. Parents stick digital devices into the hands of toddlers or plop them in front of TV screens with little or no thought about the adverse effects prolonged screen time can have on the developing brain.

Limited time is spent reading or conversing with young children, and consequently, many little ones start school with huge language deficits. Children do not get ample sleep, resulting in a myriad of problems, such as being prone to infectious diseases, becoming easily agitated, having issues with attentiveness, etc. Now more than ever, parents should function with intentionality when it comes to raising their children. When I see a family out together for a meal, and the children are well-behaved, I know that's the result of painstaking work at home. It's not easy to teach children to have good manners or behave appropriately in a variety of settings, but the Bible clearly indicates that this should be done. Proverbs 29:15 (CEV) states, "The rod and rebuke give wisdom, but a child left to himself brings shame to his mother." A more modern rendering of that same verse states, "Correct your children, and they will be wise; children out of control disgrace their mothers."

How many of us have been to a restaurant and seen a child who is out of control? The adults at the table are yelling or turning red from embarrassment. It's a bad scene. Not only is the misbehaving child disturbing his own family's peace of mind and ruining their evening out, but the bad behavior also impacts others in the surrounding area. What you do when training your children should be deliberate, always keeping in the forefront of your mind the long view, your ultimate goals, and objectives for your children. For example, if you want your children to grow up to be courteous people who are highly respectful of diversity among people, that will take a lot of work on your part. If you think it's important to teach your children empathy for others, then you must be empathetic.

Leaders in the highest political, corporate, and sometimes even religious circles may not be good role models of empathy or other positive traits for children. Leaders vary in their character, convictions, and morals. First and foremost, your children are watching your behavior. Make sure you lead by example. When you and your children observe bad behavior, take the time to discuss how Jesus would view that behavior. Ask your children what would be a more God-honoring way of behaving in that situation. You should also be quick to call attention to behavior that is reminiscent of Jesus' actions.

Right is right, and wrong is wrong. How children respond to right and wrong is a function of what they're exposed to through their families and the many other influences in their lives.

Parenting requires so much more than ensuring children are clothed, fed, and educated. I think it bears repeating: children are messages that we will send to a time we'll never see. What kind of messages will your children be delivering as a result of your diligence or benign neglect? By parenting God's way, we can confidently leave the messaging to the Lord because He knows how to best equip our children for the future demands we could never anticipate. God will help with the critically important endeavor of raising children who are prepared to step into the future. He has the Blueprint for properly raising children. God is an almighty architect and a master builder. He knows how to build boys and girls into men and women for His glory. As adults, we should seek to follow His plan. Keeping Christ in the center of our thoughts, words, and deeds will help guide and direct us to train children in the way they should go on a daily basis, focusing on their body, soul, and spirit in the process.

FOUR

Child-Centered vs. CHRIST-Centered Child-Rearing

This chapter puts a spotlight on two specific child-rearing philosophies, child-centered and CHRIST-centered, and provides a number of reasons why I believe one philosophy is the better one to have as the underlying, fundamental rationale that governs your thoughts, words, and deeds as you raise your children in today's challenging times. A person's philosophy about child rearing generally revolves around a set of principles an individual believes will result in success; these could be the principles set forth in Scripture or principles that are espoused by noted child psychologists or highly regarded experts on family matters. A parenting style is the means by which parents try to reach their goals for their children. These are the methods used in the day-to-day aspects of bringing up children.

Parenting styles and philosophies with regard to raising children abound today. Some examples include hyper-parenting, hypo-parenting, traditional/neo-traditional parenting, millennial parenting, and divergent parenting. Should you have a deep interest in exploring these parenting styles, especially relating to the pros and cons of each one, I highly recommend James M. Pedersen's book, *The Rise of the Millennial Parents: Parenting*

Yesterday and Today.[1] The content is invaluable because all these parenting approaches exist in society today, and your children will encounter children whose lives are the result of their parents' approach to parenting, among a variety of other factors. For example, hyper-parenting parents hover around their children constantly, and they're involved in even the minutest of decisions in their lives. Within this category of parenting, you'll find the designations: Blackhawk parents, commando parents, curling parents, groupie parents, helicopter parents, investment parents, lawnmower parents, and more. I was stunned to read about the sheer number of distinguishable parenting approaches that exist today, and the types of parents I previously cited are just the ones that fall into the hyper-parenting category. Perhaps what you just read gives you a taste of the smorgasbord of parenting approaches that exist today. What approach will you use? What will be the underlying child-rearing philosophy that informs your choice of a suitable parenting style?

Perhaps you would like to see various parenting styles on full display; then I suggest that you view the reality show ParentTest[2], which premiered on ABC towards the end of 2022 and concluded in early 2023. The hosts, Ali Wentworth and parenting expert Dr. Adolph Brown, co-facilitated an absolutely intriguing show designed to pit various parenting styles against one another in a competition to crown America's most effective parenting style. Twelve diverse families were put under the microscope as the viewing audience, and the other parents engaged in the competition watched each family navigate a variety of challenging scenarios. The titles of the scenarios included: High Dive, Unexpected Pick-Up, Rock Climb, Stranger Danger, Fine Dining, Facts of Life, Scary Situation, and more. The varied approaches used by the Helicopter, Traditional, Child-led, Intensive, High Achievement, Natural, Routine, Negotiation, Free Range, Strict, Disciplined, and New Age parents fostered conversations about how each family unit operates. The hosts moderated the discussions to maintain a judgment-free space for the parents to share their ideas. While the parents definitely have conflicting views about how to raise children, they all share the same common goal of building solid family relationships to foster emotionally whole children who are able to navigate their world. Isn't that a goal most well-meaning parents share?

Some approaches to parenting are transitory and popular for only a short time; nevertheless, the impact on the lives of children is long-lasting. I'll provide one example from James Pedersen's book, *The Rise of Millennial Parents: Parenting Yesterday and Today.* Blackhawk parents is the designation given to parents who function like the Blackhawk assault helicopters used by the US military to wage attacks against enemies. From these parents' perspective, they must protect their children from anything that might be unpleasant, critical, or something they deem a threat to them. So, whether it's doctors, teachers, neighbors, or even other family members who are doling out criticism or unpleasant tasks, these parents try to step in and intervene in all sorts of ways, some as unethical as doing their children's homework for them and then becoming belligerent if someone accuses them of doing it. Believe me, as a career educator, I have encountered a few Blackhawk parents in my time, and they can be quite challenging! How can a child learn perseverance, diligence, resilience, and a myriad of other critical traits if an adult is doing their work for them? And can they learn to be honest if their parents lie about doing their work?

Let's start with the premise that the vast majority of parents desire to raise well-adjusted, academically proficient, socially savvy, and community-focused children. After all, what parent looks into the eyes of their newborn baby and then at their growing young child and sees a future drug dealer, thief, sexual predator, murderer, con man, or alcoholic? Parents almost always envision their children accomplishing more than they've been able to achieve themselves, hoping their children obtain far more lucrative and prestigious positions than they had during the course of their own lives. If wishes came true with the blink of an eye or three clicks of one's heels, parenting would be "easy breezy." But that's definitely not the case, and it seems the hard work of parenting gets harder and harder as times change and questionable trends become more pervasive.

There are distinct philosophical differences between child-centered and CHRIST-centered child-rearing:

- Child-centered child-rearing encourages children and/or parents to think that family decisions, whether they are large or small, revolve around what the children want. This approach prioritizes the children's interests and demands even above parental wisdom.
- CHRIST-centered child-rearing encourages the children to put their trust in an unfailing God. Parents faithfully lift Jesus Christ as the supreme and righteous role model in all things: obedience, humility of heart, meekness and lowliness of mind, selflessness, etc. Choices made for children are made in light of what God wants for them, which is clearly depicted on the pages of Scripture, and not exclusively what they desire for themselves.

Children's whims and fancies clearly reign supreme in homes where a child-centered philosophy is the order of the day. In these homes, children determine menus based on their food preferences, whether they'll attend church and/or Sunday School as a result of their desire to "sleep in" or participate in some alternate activity the child deems more appealing. The children dictate policy about what clothes and shoes they'll wear, given what's in vogue, or how much screen time they'll engage in, and on and on it goes. These children call the shots in their homes. The parents' wisdom and good judgment fall prey to their desire to appease their children. Lines of parental authority are not well defined but blurred. The children seem to be the real power brokers in the relationship, as they are continually getting what they want. And what is the result? Spoiled children who fail miserably in the area of social-emotional learning. In many instances, the character issues that develop over time have a major impact on their academic achievements as well.

A parent's overall child-rearing philosophy will typically sway them towards a particular parenting style. Parents would do well to give intentional, prayerful consideration to their overarching philosophy of child-rearing and the parenting style that will best support their philosophical choice. Because CHRIST-centered child-rearing clearly keeps God at the center of all things, and what is written in His Word is prevalent in decision-making, that is the firmest foundation on which to build your children's lives. Jesus Christ is the Rock of Ages, and His ways stand the test of time. Trends may come and go, but raising your children in accordance with Biblical principles builds a rock-solid foundation that can withstand the assaults of the adversities, frustrations, uncertainties, and disappointments that will most assuredly pummel your children at some point in their lives. Parenting approaches that better align with a Christ-centered focus will result in far fewer negative consequences in the short and long term. The following quote appeared in *Our Daily Bread* on April 17, 2015: "Jesus is the best foundation upon which to build a solid life."[3]

When the choice of how to raise children is whether one should build on the shifting sands of current philosophical trends or the bedrock principles contained in God's Word, don't agonize about the choice you should make. God's instructions are in His Word to set and keep things straight. When we allow the Scriptures to be our blueprint and our guide day by day, our lives more easily align with God's will for us. When we fully recognize and embrace the fact that God's plan for us is good, as stated in Jeremiah 29:11, why risk deviating from the wisdom of God's Word? As a parent, make sure you go with what is time-tested and true. Take courage from the promise in Isaiah 40:8, "The grass withers, the flower fades, but the word of our God stands forever." Not only does the word of God stand forever, but God will stand by you forever. The Lord will never fail or forsake you when it comes to providing any help you'll need to raise your children in a CHRIST-centered way.

FIVE

Character is the Key

The American Heritage Dictionary of the English Language defines character as the combination of mental characteristics and behavior that distinguishes a person or group, moral strength, and integrity.[1] The King James version of the Bible never uses the word "character." However, integrity is used numerous times in that particular translation of God's Word. The importance of integrity is clearly seen in Proverbs 11:3, "The integrity of the upright shall guide them, but the perverseness of transgressors shall destroy them." A simple definition of character that's easy to teach young children is doing right even when you don't like it. So then, a person with integrity or good character has the ability to do the right thing, even under pressure or in times of crisis, distress, or despair. Of course, possessing good character and functioning in the previously mentioned way is much easier said than done.

Character development in children does not occur because well-meaning adults want it to or because they take time to write down elaborate goals. Sad to say, many parents invest much time and money to set their children up for the world's definition of success. Some young children will cheat just to take home one more piece of hardware or some unmerited award because their parents push them relentlessly. Or worse yet, many well-meaning adult leaders will give a trophy to every child, even to a lazy and undeserving one, so that no one's feelings get hurt. In my role as a career educator, I have seen some children learn early on that certain achievements please their parents and others. These children scheme and manipulate and do other unseemly things to bring home a title or achieve a victory. Titles and achievements have their place, but what really matters is how gracious, honest, compassionate, and loving our children are becoming. Character is what counts in God's eyes. Godly character is the key to unlocking God's blessings in our lives and the lives of our children.

This chapter, Character is the Key, will be a substantive one because, as Emanuel James Rohn says, "Character is a quality that embodies many important traits such as integrity, courage, perseverance, confidence, and wisdom."[2] Rohn, a true "rags to riches" phenomenon, was a highly esteemed entrepreneur, author, and motivational speaker. He died at the age of 79 in 2009, but for more than 40 years prior to his passing, Rohn was considered a guru, easily one of the most influential speakers and authors for anyone seeking guidance on ways to be successful in the area of personal development. Rohn goes on to say about character, "Character isn't something you were born with and can't change, like your fingerprints. It's something you must take responsibility for forming."[3] During a child's formative years, parents and like-minded adults must painstakingly teach values to help develop the character that will pave the way for a successful future, as well as enable children to avoid the tragic results that ensue when people lack character.

Instilling godly character in children is a pursuit that requires dedicated parents, grandparents, teachers, caregivers, and church workers to maximize their efforts on a daily basis. Here is what Heraclitus, a 6th-century Greek philosopher who lived in Ephesus, said about character development: "Good character is not formed in a week or a month. It is created little by little, day by day. Protracted and patient effort is needed to develop good character."[4]

Intentional, diligent care should be taken to capitalize on character development because parents and other concerned adults are well aware of its lifelong importance.

The ultimate goal is to help children do the right thing, in the right way, at the right time, with the right attitude, even when they don't want to. Nowadays, it's quite challenging to discern what is right and what is wrong in a world where countless ideologies abound. Current thinking on any given issue can be so radically different depending on who or what you rely on as your principal information source. That is why it's so important to turn to the Bible for answers to life's questions. We can have confidence that God's Word is a guide to eternal truth on matters of life and godliness.

Godly character consists of numerous traits that we see on vivid display in the life of Jesus. Jesus' character is the "gold standard." Helping our children reflect His integrity in their lives should be a deep desire of our hearts. The following distinguishable features or characteristics do not form an exhaustive list, but will be discussed in this chapter:

- Obedience
- Reverence
- Wisdom
- Faith
- Honesty
- Patience
- Thankfulness
- Self-Control
- Tenderheartedness
- Orderliness
- Purity
- Forgiveness

OBEDIENCE

Obedience is doing what one is told to do and submitting to authority or law. An easy-to-remember definition of obedience for young children is "doing things God's way."

True obedience involves doing what an authority wants immediately, respectfully, and completely. This requires submission of the person's will to those in charge. It is God who commands obedience.

An excellent example of obedience is Abraham's response to God in Genesis 22:1-18 when He asked Abraham to sacrifice his son, Isaac. The Bible speaks about obedience to parents, the pastor, governmental authorities, the boss on the job, etc. [See Ephesians 6:1-3,5; Hebrews 13:17; 1 Peter 2:13,14, 17].

The supreme model of obedience is our Lord Jesus Christ. He obeyed the Father in all things. He was obedient unto death to provide salvation for humankind. [See Philippians 2:8]

Obedience to God and all God-ordained authorities must start in the home. No one wants to obey. Our sinful nature makes us prone to rebel, to disobey. A child who is not taught to obey in the home is likely to have problems in school when teachers request obedience in the classroom.

Some typical examples of obedience include:

- Doing chores without prompting or excessive prodding.
- Responding to a specific request from a parent or teacher, the first time the request is made.
- Following classroom rules.
- Adhering to the house rule of no cell phones at the table during meals.
- Complying with the designated curfew to arrive back home or the time for lights out.

Obedience comes as a result of training. Children must be trained from an early age to obey. Training combines teaching with requiring the child to do what has been taught. Training involves doling out praise and applying penalties as appropriate. How do your children respond when you call them? Do they acknowledge you by saying, "Yes, Daddy," and come immediately, or do they ignore you and act like you never called them at all? You are involved in a negative training process if you allow your child to get away with not responding to a clear command the first time it is spoken. By repeating yourself over and over again, you're reinforcing and encouraging disobedience. This may sound harsh, but you're training your child unto unrighteousness. Remember, if it's been tolerated, it's been taught.

When you speak to a child in a way that requires a response, you should expect obedience. Call him once, and he doesn't come---he's made a choice to disobey, and that's on him. Call him twice, and he doesn't come---you're making a choice to ignore the disobedience consciously, and that's on you. Truth be told, if you repeat yourself enough times, you're neglecting to train your child in the way she should go; instead, you're fostering the habit of being disobedient in your life and your child's life. We are what we repeatedly do.

Commands or requests should be clear, and children should be required to respond the first time the command or request is given. For example, "Johnny, please clean up your room now" should be met with the respectful response, "Yes, Mommy," and he starts the task immediately. Anything short of that is disobedience, and adults who allow children to get away with chronic disobedience do them a tremendous disservice. Of course, a child may ask permission to delay getting started on a particular request, but it's the parent's prerogative to say yes to their reasonable request. As the parent, you should not get into a negotiation with a child to get something done, nor should you bribe a child or offer specific rewards to motivate the child to get a task done. Children are not the ones to dictate policy to parents, teachers, or anyone else in authority. They are the ones who are called to obedience.

To facilitate obedience, you can establish verbal authority by:
1. Calling the child's name.
2. Establishing eye contact, even if it means bending down to the child's eye level.
3. Providing a simple, clear-cut command or request (in a normal tone of voice).
4. Speaking once.

Obedience is the principal parental training objective from day one to five years of age. A child who has been trained to be obedient will be easier to interact with from ages six to twelve years old when you're concentrating on the full gamut of character development in earnest. From ages thirteen to eighteen, the task is to help children internalize various character qualities and apply what has been taught on a consistent basis in their daily activities.

Training a child to be obedient requires diligent work, but it's well worth the effort. Obedient children are not only pleasant to interact with, but they are also happy and secure because they have clear-cut boundaries to respond to.

Here are some practical suggestions for fostering obedience:

- Discuss the definition of obedience, providing age-appropriate examples. Post the definition of obedience in a prominent place as a reminder. Ensure your child can explain what obedience means in their own words.
- Read and discuss as a family, Bible stories such as Noah building the ark (Genesis 6-8), Abraham offering Isaac (Genesis 22), and the march around Jericho (Joshua 6).

- Discuss the list of blessings that result from obedience that are presented in Deuteronomy 28:1-14. Look at Deuteronomy 28:15-68 for the consequences of disobedience. The blessings of obedience and the curses of disobedience are also presented in Leviticus 26.
- Memorize poems that contain an obedience theme. (See Appendix B).
- Read books where obedience and disobedience are in full view and discuss the consequences of the behavior.
- As a family project, make a list of all the blessings that have come into the lives of family members and friends when they obeyed God.
- Routinely praise your children by citing the specifics of the behavior when they are obedient. Remind them that their obedience pleases and blesses God, you, and others.
- Devise a system of rewards when genuine obedience is carried out.
- Point out examples of "real world" obedience and disobedience and discuss the consequences that came about as a result of the choice to obey or disobey.

Parents, do yourself a huge favor by teaching your children to obey the first time you ask them to do something. Do you want to be the red-faced parent who screams out of your pent-up frustration and desperation, "You better get off that slide right now!" How many times have you seen parents resort to shouting after they've told their child multiple times that it's time to go? Do you want to be the parent who snatches your child off the slide after they proceed to ignore you one more time? That kind of parental lack of control is never pretty. Worse yet, do you want your child to ignore your clear request to come off the slide, and upon ignoring you, she tumbles off and gets injured? Consider this: dogs learn to sit, fetch, carry, and do other things when they are trained to obey. There are books and schools devoted to teaching pet owners what to do and not do to help foster the pet's obedience. I truly believe children are far more intelligent than any pet. If a dog can learn to obey, surely a son or daughter can learn to obey.

I think it bears repeating that obedience is the result of painstaking, determined training by parents, grandparents, teachers, and other concerned adults. Of course, it's easier to be haphazard or lackadaisical when it comes to teaching children to obey, but that approach will come back to haunt you and hurt your children in the end. When your child learns to carry out your requests or the requests of someone in authority immediately, completely, and respectfully, you, your child, and others will be blessed. I was reminded of an example of obedience that occurred years ago in my own family when my college-age daughter was concerned that her toddler-age little brother was headed directly toward our busy street. She exclaimed, "Don't you want me to run after him? "Instead of telling her yes, I said his name and uttered one word: STOP. My son froze in his tracks and looked right at me. My daughter marveled at his obedient response. As I told his sister then, and I share with you now, obedience can be a matter of life and death. Children must be taught to obey. Children who chronically disobey their parents cause all sorts of difficulties for themselves and their families, from embarrassment to unnecessary injury, inconvenience, and expense. All the effort devoted to teaching children to obey will be well worth it. Put in the time when your children are small, and the benefits from obedient behavior will become clearly evident as the years pass by and your children mature. If Jesus was obedient to His Father's will, shouldn't we help our children to be obedient to the will of their parents and others who may be in authority?

A Prayer For Help

Dear Lord, even though I find it hard to obey You, yet, by Your grace, I can be obedient. When I obey, blessings always follow. Please help me to be a good example in the area of obedience. Teach me the best approaches to use with my children so they learn the importance of obedience. I know it is crucial that they learn to carry out the requests of those in authority immediately, completely, and respectfully. Help me to help my children.

In Jesus' name. Amen.

REVERENCE

Reverence is a feeling of deep respect mixed with wonder, fear, and love. A simple definition of reverence is being amazed by who God is and what He can do.

Proverbs 1:7 (Amp) "The reverent and worshipful fear of the Lord is the beginning and the principal and choice part of knowledge [its starting point and its essence], but fools despise skillful and godly wisdom, instruction, and discipline."

Children must be taught deep respect for the Lord, as respect doesn't come naturally. Respect for God will also produce respect for others, especially God-ordained authorities such as parents, teachers, church and government leaders, and employers. We should strive to respect all people because we're all made in the image and likeness of God. We're all precious souls for whom Christ died. All property, our own and that of others, should be respected because our Creator ultimately creates all things. Reverence, like all character traits, is best caught rather than taught. Children are always watching to see if parents and the other adults in their circles of acquaintance respect God, members of the church, teachers, employers, police officers, and people who are different than themselves.

They are like sponges and will soak up and repeat disrespectful teasing, name-calling, cursing, gossiping, and the like. Sometimes, negative, and disrespectful influences come from social media sites, TV programs, music, movies, books, and fashion, even "so-called" leaders. Point out examples of disrespect to your children, and when they're the offenders, shut it down immediately. Instead, replace any negative influences with positive ones. Young children should be given the correct response immediately and asked to repeat it. For older children, ask what a more polite or respectful way to say or do something might be. Promote silence as an acceptable alternative whenever appropriate. Even silence is far better than a constant stream of negative and disrespectful commentary. In your home, speech should be designed to build up and edify people, never tear anyone down, and that includes conversations between siblings.

Some examples of reverential actions/respect for others are:

- Standing up during the reading of God's Word.
- Not texting during the worship service.
- Not talking during prayer or the sermon.
- Not walking around at various points in the church service.
- Muting the TV during family grace for meals.
- Saying grace in public settings.
- Wearing garments with Scripture verses or positive sayings.
- Teaching children to respect their elders by using an appropriate title with their names, acknowledging their

presence by speaking courteously to them, and doing kind deeds for them.

- Listening attentively while someone else is speaking, not talking over them, or cutting them off mid-sentence.
- Not rolling your eyes when someone irritates you.
- Refraining from using profanity and name-calling.

Practical suggestions for cultivating reverence include:

- Discuss the definition of reverence, providing age-appropriate examples. Post the definition of reverence in a prominent place as a reminder. Ensure your child can define reverence in her or his own words.
- Identify Bible verses (use a concordance to assist you) about reverence and encourage your children to memorize them.
- Do not allow children to have side conversations, scroll through phone messages, or engage in other activities while the family is doing family devotions, having a meal together, or engaging in serious conversation.
- Discourage children from walking around during prayers, the pastor's sermon, choir selections, or other parts of the worship service.
- Memorize poems that depict the importance of respect. (See Appendix B).
- Refrain from hollering or screaming at a child, especially in public.
- Make sure T-shirt slogans are uplifting; for example, "If you don't stand for something, you'll fall for anything." Avoid degrading slogans, for example, "Grandma's Little Devil."
- Vigilantly monitor music, TV programs, reading materials, social media posts, podcasts, movies, and so forth for objectionable content. If something is banned in your home

as irreverent or disrespectful, replace it with an acceptable alternative or suggested option.

- Point out disrespectful behavior and discuss why that type of behavior displeases the Lord. Share Scripture verses whenever applicable.
- Don't "badmouth" or insult your spouse or other relatives, your child's teachers, church leaders, neighbors, government leaders, people with physical or emotional challenges, or people of a different race or religion. Children have ears and will mimic you.

Respect for God and others, especially people different from ourselves, seems to be quite out of step these days. Do not allow your family to be swept away in the current riptide of insults, profanity, hate speech, and so forth. A woman very much my senior once said to me that even the most aggravating, disrespectful person is still a precious soul for whom Christ died. That really helped to put a person's worth clearly in focus for me, and I found myself inclined to view the person differently and, consequently, speak about them differently. We all want to be valued and respected, and treating others as we wish to be treated is something God desires for us to do. It goes without saying that parents must be good examples of respectful behavior if they want their children to be respectful.

Start by giving God the honor and reverence He's due in your home. Continue your respectful behavior while you're in the household of faith, interacting with God's people. Try to be mindful of the respect you show other people who may not share your views. It will be easier for your children to develop the same type of respectful behavior they see you modeling.

A Prayer For Help

Almighty God, help me to give You the honor that You richly deserve. Correct me when I speak to or about others in ways that are not pleasing to You. I want to be a positive influence on my children, so they learn to view You with reverential awe and show respect to all the precious souls for whom You died.

Amen.

WISDOM

Wisdom can be defined as having knowledge and good judgment based on experience. Sarah Young writes about wisdom in her quintessential devotional, *Jesus Always*, as "the ability to make good decisions based on knowledge and experience."[5] A working definition of wisdom for a young child could be thinking God's way.

To think what God thinks, we must know what His Word says. The book of Proverbs is a practical book dealing with the art of living, and it bases wisdom solidly on the fear of the Lord (Proverbs 1:7). Proverbs teaches what God thinks about foolishness or the foolish person. Of course, a fool is quite the opposite of a wise individual. Proverbs provide a clear contrast of these two types of people.

It's important to take the time to teach our children what judicious thinking entails and why it's important to cultivate this type of thinking to avoid needless negative consequences in our lives. As God's people, we should be as adept at spotting con artists and scammers as a trained bank teller is at spotting counterfeit money. That takes time and training, just like obtaining wisdom and then imparting wisdom to gullible children. In John 1:1, we read that God was at the beginning, and if He was at the beginning, we can rest assured that God knows all we'll ever need to know. Be sure you're acquainted with what godly wisdom looks like in day-to-day situations. That's what God's Word will show you. The seven attributes of godly wisdom are listed in James 3:17. The Living Bible translation presents that verse this way, "But the wisdom that comes from above is first of all pure and full of quiet gentleness. Then it's peace-loving and courteous. It allows discussion and is willing to yield to others; it is full of mercy and good deeds. It is wholehearted and sincere." The Lord clearly tells us what we need to know and do, or not do, to be wise and discerning people. Within the pages of the Bible, wisdom and folly are clearly on view for everyone to see. The wisdom that followers of Jesus should seek is reflected in Christ's character. "Seek, and ye shall find..." (Matthew 7:7).

Some common examples of wisdom include:

- Paying attention to health and safety warning signals.
- Staying away from negative influences.
- Heeding the warnings of people in authority.
- Asking for help when confused or overwhelmed.
- Avoiding addictive substances.
- Engaging others in conversation who are wiser about particular situations.
- Following the advice of experts gleaned from various sources.
- Reading about and talking through various courses of action before making a major decision.
- Noting the negative consequences that happen when a person engages in foolish behavior.
- Studying the positive results that happen from wise choices
- Thinking through potential responses to challenging situations before encountering them.

Here are some practical suggestions for promoting wisdom:

- Post the definition of wisdom in a prominent place. Discuss the meaning of the word, ensuring your child has a working definition of wisdom.
- Memorize wisdom Scripture verses: Proverbs 4:7; James 3:17; James 1:5; 1 Kings 3:9; Luke 2:52; Isaiah 33:6; Romans 11:33a; 1 Corinthians 2:5; 1 Corinthians 3:19a.
- Use the book of Proverbs to make a list contrasting the characteristics of the foolish person and the wise person.
- Memorize poems with wisdom themes. (See Appendix B)
- Read books featuring characters who embody wisdom. Discuss how the character's wise actions were a benefit to them personally and to others.
- Identify or ask your children to identify "people in the news" who have acted wisely or foolishly. Ask them to cite specific examples of their wise or foolish behavior. Comment on the results of their foolish or wise behavior.
- Praise your children when they use good judgment. Find opportunities to share their good judgment with others.
- Discuss "what if" situations before they happen so you can get an idea of what your child's thinking would be. Cite wise or wiser choices for the situation when appropriate.
- Determine clear-cut boundaries for your children so they know what the limits are. Present Scriptural reasons for your decisions.

Wisdom seems to be in such short supply these days. Foolish behavior is so prevalent, and I'm not talking about children who are inexperienced in life matters and can be expected to be foolish.

I'm concerned about the foolish behavior exhibited by adults. Some foolish behavior is downright dangerous, like texting and driving, leaving guns unsecured in homes, ignoring science-based evidence that promotes healthy and safe living, allowing children to be unsupervised in risky situations, and falling prey to various scams. God's advice about the important issues of life will keep us out of trouble. Adults do well when the pursuit of wisdom is one of their main goals in life. Children profit greatly from observing wise adults. It's easier for them to follow in their footsteps because they see adults who are not only well-informed about the value of wisdom, but they observe lives that are abundantly blessed as a result of wise actions.

A Prayer For Help

I know I need more wisdom when it comes to being the best parent I can be. I admit it is sometimes hard for me to go against popular thinking, but I want to improve in this area of exercising wisdom. God, help me to make wise decisions and take wise actions on a day-to-day basis.

In Jesus' name, Amen.

FAITH

Faith is belief in God's promises, trust, and confidence in God. Very simply put, faith is believing God will do what He says He will do. For a young child, a helpful definition of faith is believing in God no matter what.

Faith is described in Hebrews 11:1 as the substance of things hoped for, the evidence of things not seen. Today, voices are very loud, at times screaming at us that we should believe in ourselves, trust others, and have confidence in our position or our accumulated wealth. Our faith should be centered in God, in His provision of salvation through Jesus Christ, and in His provision for our daily needs. Hebrews 11:6 states, "But without faith it is impossible to please Him, for he who comes to God must believe that He is, and that He is a rewarder of those who diligently seek Him."

Some examples of faith include:

- Believing there will be Christmas presents for children after parental job loss just before the holidays.
- Providing tithes and offerings to the church during financially challenging times.
- Believing that family, church members, and friends will be a support system during a health crisis, the loss of a loved one, or other challenging times.
- Working toward a challenging goal, believing it can be achieved.
- Believing that the logistics related to a complicated relocation will work out favorably.
- Trusting God to provide needed medical and financial assistance after a serious diagnosis.
- Believing that something good can result from a major disappointment or tragic event.

There will be times in your family's life journey when jobs will be lost, promotions will result in relocation, loved ones will get very sick, and some will pass away, relatives or friends will fall on hard times and need help, people who mean so much to the family will move away, or worse yet, some unresolved issue will be the conduit to a seemingly irreconcilable difference. This is when the rubber of life's hardships, challenges, perplexities, and opportunities meets the road of faith, usually a road less traveled. The Bible tells us to walk by faith and not by sight, yet that seems almost impossible to do. Human nature wants everything spelled out for us. We need to see it to believe it rather than believe it to see it. God's ways are never our ways; they seem to be polar opposite to the ways we feel comfortable getting things done. It's imperative that we know God's promises and truly believe He will more than deliver on His promises. Grumbling and complaining about present bad circumstances and expressing doubt and fear on a continual basis do not pave the way for God to work on our behalf. Children tend to be incredibly trusting until well-meaning adults teach them by example to be doubtful and cynical. Praying steadfastly and repeating God's promises as part of your prayers build confidence and show God you trust Him to take care of the situation. Allow your children to enter into this sacred time of prayer. You might be thinking, what if God doesn't answer my prayer request the way I ask Him to, or I'd like Him to? Won't my children begin to doubt God when that happens? You need not worry about God's reputation as it relates to answering prayers. So, what if God doesn't answer the request to your liking? Know this: God always has a better plan. He is infinitely wiser than we are because He knows the beginning from the end. When God answers a prayer differently, let your children know that it is His choice. Look for the ways that God's answer to prayers is better than your requests. Point out that fact to your children.

I am particularly fond of a song by Babbie Mason called *Trust His Heart*.[6] You can ask "Alexa" to play the song or check it out on YouTube, but the chorus is as follows:

God is too wise to be mistaken,
God is too good to be unkind
So if you don't understand
If you can't see His Plan
If you can't trace His hand
Trust His heart.

Countless faith stories in the Bible can stir your heart and encourage your faith. Become familiar with the little boy who shared his five loaves and two fish with Jesus (John 6:1- 14), the woman who touched the hem of Jesus' garment (Luke 8:43-48), and Jairus' plea for his sick daughter's life (Luke 8:41, 42, 49-56). In each situation, the outcome seemed to be a foregone conclusion, but active faith in God proved what it says in Luke 1:37, "For with God nothing will be impossible."

That voice in your head may be saying, "My faith is small." Faith typically starts small, like the barely visible first flicker of candlelight, and as it continues to guide your actions, it burns brighter and brighter for all to see, like the large bonfire that is visible from a distance. A minuscule amount of faith is all that is needed if it is sincere faith in God. Believe what Jesus says in Matthew 17:20, "... if you have faith as a mustard seed, you will say to this mountain, 'Move from here to there,' and it will move, and nothing will be impossible for you." Have you ever seen the size of a mustard seed? It's tiny. I'd describe the size of a mustard seed to be similar to the size of the head on a straight pin. So again, I say, don't worry about the size of your faith; just keep exercising it on a regular basis. God is totally trustworthy, and as you believe He is a faithful promise keeper; He won't let you down. God is the author and perfecter of your faith. Believe that in your heart of hearts and say resoundingly, Glory hallelujah! AMEN!

Suggestions to foster faith include:

- Post the definition of faith in a prominent place, and then, after you discuss the meaning of the word, ensure your child has a working definition of faith.
- Pray together as a family for specific requests. Record the requests and the answers to your prayers.
- Attend prayer meetings at your church.
- Review Luke 7:1-10, which provides an example of the Centurion's faith in Jesus' power to perform a miracle

through His spoken word. Read the story as a family. With young children, you might have them act out the story. For older children, you might have them state how they think the Centurion's faith pleased God.

- Have your child draw a picture showing what faith means to him or her. Display the picture in a prominent place under the definition of faith.
- Memorize faith-themed poems (See Appendix B).
- Read books or view movies with inspiring faith stories. Discuss how the story is helpful in growing faith.
- Use the people of faith listed in Hebrews 11 to develop a "Faith Record." In one column, put the Bible character's name. In the second column, tell how the Bible character displayed his faith, or her faith. In the third column, write how God rewarded their faith.
- Have older children do interviews with church leaders, members of the congregation, relatives, and friends to find out ways they put their faith in God and how God rewarded their faith.
- Develop a "Faithfulness Record" in which you write down how God has been faithful to your family and others you may know.

Faith pleases God. Faith unlocks incredible blessings in the lives of those who believe God's promises are yea and amen. God always proves Himself faithful. Trust God with your whole heart and lean not to your own understanding. Give God a chance to work in your situation. What is best for you may not be what you want, or what you want may not occur as quickly as you'd like, but that does not negate the fact that God is righteous in all the works that He does. Have faith in God, and you will be blessed, far above anything you could ever imagine or envision for your life, for the lives of your children, and for the lives of other people you love.

A Prayer For Help

Dear God, You always prove yourself faithful, even when I fail to believe that things will really be okay. Lord, help my unbelief in those areas that pose a struggle for me. Strengthen my faith walk so my children can follow in my footsteps and become the people of faith You'd like them to be.

Amen.

HONESTY

Honesty can be described as refraining from lying, cheating, stealing, or misrepresenting. An easy definition for children to remember is "having truthful words and ways."

In our everyday circumstances, we will encounter dishonest people. Some individuals have become accustomed to lying and cheating in many areas of life. There are those folks who tout alternate facts and conspiracy theories as truth and almost dare anyone to dispute what they are saying and what they believe to be true. The temptation to lie or exaggerate is on display in people's lives when they're trying to avoid getting into some sort of trouble, or they're trying to obtain a more favorable outcome for themselves. God's way is to tell the truth even when it may be the more difficult thing to do.

Honesty pleases God. In Proverbs 12:22, we see, "Lying lips are an abomination to the Lord, but those who deal truthfully are his delight." It's always the better choice to please God rather than others or yourself. One of the duties of the Christian is to be honest. Ephesians 4:25 states, "Therefore, putting away lying, 'Let each one of you speak truth with his neighbor,' for we are members of one another." Truth is the basis for trust. Without trust, relationships falter and ultimately fail.

We should speak the truth as we engage in any conversation with others. Our aim should be to speak the truth in love. Teach your children to tell the truth, constantly stressing the importance of being an honest and trustworthy individual. Our commitment to the importance of honesty in our interactions with others and our positive example are probably the most powerful forces at play when teaching this particular character trait to our children. Some things are better caught rather than taught.

Some everyday examples of honesty include:

- Not cheating on a test.
- Telling the truth when asked if the child broke an object or broke a house rule.
- Admitting that the money set aside for the Sunday School offering was actually used to buy candy.
- Letting a parent know a friend stole something from a classmate's locker.
- Going back to pay for the item that was not included by the cashier.
- Not pretending to be sick to get out of something you really don't want to do.
- Not asking someone to say you're unavailable when you'd rather not speak to that person.

Suggestions to cultivate honesty:

- Start with the definition of honesty. Keep the definition visible for a while and discuss the meaning of honesty a few times. Make sure your child can explain the character trait accurately.
- Encourage Scripture memorization that builds truthfulness, for example, Ephesians 6:14 (NLT), "Stand your ground,

putting on the belt of truth and the body armor of God's righteousness."

- Make sure your own life is an example of truthfulness. If you tell your child there are no funds to buy the thing they've been pestering you about, when money is available for the purchase you don't want to make, you're lying, and you provide a negative example.

- Point out real-world examples of honesty and dishonesty. Look at any consequences, good or bad, that result from the behavior under review.

- Praise honesty in your children and others.

- Read and discuss stories or current events where the character quality of honesty is clearly depicted. Point out the challenges of being honest and the outcomes.

- Memorize poems that highlight honesty. (See Appendix B)

- Reduce punishment for offenses when the child tells the truth immediately and completely when asked if she has not actually been caught "red-handed."

- Make the punishment for lying far exceed any momentary benefit or satisfaction gained by it.

- NEVER accuse a child of lying unless you have absolute proof. Refrain from making an accusation based only on circumstantial evidence. When you suspect a child has lied, prayerfully ask God to expose the lie or convict the child's heart and bring him to repentance.

We live in an era where people make up and then boldly proclaim their alternate facts as truth. Ignorance of the truth can have deadly consequences. People truly are destroyed by a lack of knowledge. Intimate knowledge of the eternal truth that is clearly presented in God's Word will be a safety net during these tumultuous times. This is not the time to be gullible and uninformed. Now is the time to be truthful and be able to discern truth from error easily.

A Prayer For Help

Dear God, forgive me when I am dishonest. I want to be a better role model of truthfulness for my children. You are the way, the truth, and the life. Help me to make the truth, Your truth, an important part of my life. In Jesus' name.

Amen.

PATIENCE

Patience is the willingness to put up with waiting, pain, annoying situations, troubles, or hurts, enduring calmly without complaining or losing self-control. In her daily devotional, *Jesus Always*, Sarah Young describes patience as the ability to endure adversity calmly, not becoming upset when waiting a long time or dealing with difficult people or problems.[7] To describe this vital attribute to a young child in an easy, useful way, you can say patience is waiting upon the Lord with a happy spirit.

In our instant society, it is very easy to react to situations that demand waiting with an attitude of fretfulness. We need to learn to wait with the right attitude as God changes things. Usually, the biggest thing that must be changed is us. We need a change of heart, a change of attitude, a change of perspective. The proper perspective is always God's perspective about people, places, and things. We can learn to discern what God thinks about a matter as we read, study, and memorize His Word.

God's revelatory knowledge is available to us as we earnestly seek to obtain it. God provides the power to help us wait patiently for Him to act. Patience is developed through faithful waiting. The truth is, God has a master plan. His plans for us are ultimately for good and not for evil. God will take the most difficult circumstances that we encounter and transform our character to be stronger and better for all that we have had to endure. Let the Word of God encourage your heart as you read, "His glorious power will make you patient and strong enough to endure anything, and you will be truly happy." ~ Colossians 1:11 (CEV).

Everyday examples of patience include:
- Waiting for one's turn to be called on for a classroom activity.
- Waiting in the drive-thru without complaining about the slow service.
- Repeating the same answer several times to a question asked by an elderly person or a young child.
- Riding in the car without asking every few minutes, "Are we there yet?"
- Staying positive when someone is having a hard time learning a new concept or skill.
- Waiting for a meal to be served at a restaurant when it is short-staffed.
- Waiting for initial assistance or call backs to resolve issues of concern.

Some suggestions to nurture patience include:
- Post and discuss the definition of patience and ensure your child has a working definition of the character trait.
- Read together and discuss verses such as: James 5:8, 2 Peter 3:9, James 5:10-11a, Isaiah 53:1-12, and 1 Peter 3:17-18.
- Demonstrate patience in common everyday situations. For example, while driving in heavy traffic, don't ride the shoulder so you can cut in front of other cars.
- Come up with ideas for creative or practical ways to use waiting times when you're on line at various places like stores, the post office, or sitting in the doctor's office.

- Read and discuss the stories of Jesus, Job, Paul, and Joseph from the viewpoint of their patience.
- Cultivate patience within your own home and outside your family circle. Encourage, exhibit, and praise patience extended to little children, to people who may be sick or incapacitated, and to the elderly.
- Do projects together that take time and patience, such as baking a cake from scratch, building a robot, putting together a huge puzzle, growing a garden.
- Listen intently to someone else when they are speaking. Do not interrupt or talk over that person. Insist that your children do likewise.
- Do not grumble, fret, or complain when something needed or desired is taking far more time to come to fruition than expected. Learn to trust God with the ultimate timing of things that transpire in your life and the lives of your children.
- Journal difficult moments in your life, and then tell your children about what God taught you through a period of waiting or trouble.
- Memorize patience-themed poems (See Appendix B).
- Read books or essays where patience is exhibited and discuss the specific actions that showed the person's patience.
- Point out everyday examples of people whose patience resulted in positive outcomes or whose impatience resulted in negative outcomes.

Truth be told, few people are inclined to be patient these days. We want everything faster, with fewer errors, and let's not forget we even want fast service to come with a smile. So many fond memories can be forged by engaging in activities that require patience, like cooking meals or baking from scratch, doing puzzles, playing board games like chess, checkers, or Scrabble, or arriving 15-20 minutes before the sun comes up and waiting with eager anticipation for the beautiful sunrise to unfold. Ask any parent with adult children how fast the time flies. When little ones are young, it's time to deliberately and intentionally appreciate precious and teachable moments in the midst of the endless madness of fixing lunches, doing laundry, carting children off to various and sundry activities, or sitting anxiously in the doctor's office. Time is fleeting, and time spent with children seems to pass by all too quickly.

Patience is a very valuable safeguard to prevent tragic circumstances from occurring. A Chinese proverb is as follows: "One moment of patience may ward off disaster. One moment of impatience may ruin a life." Let that sink in for a moment and reflect on times in your life, the life of someone you know and love, or some famous person, where the words of the proverb absolutely came to pass. These are sobering truths. In the Bible, we read that tribulation works patience. Who wants to go through tribulation or adversity? That is not the choice of anyone in their right mind! Yet, as we exercise patience, God causes us and others around us to taste and see that this particular fruit of the Spirit is very good.

Make your days count for time and eternity by painstakingly and patiently teaching your children the values espoused and modeled by God Himself. With the help of the Holy Spirit, you can become a patient person.

A Prayer For Help

Almighty God, how great Thou art! Not only is Your great power and love to be admired and emulated, but so is Your great patience with Your children. Thank you for not treating us as our sins deserve. How sad when I get irritated with my children. Please help me to be a more patient person.

Patience is one of the fruit of the Spirit that I need you to cultivate in each member of our family. Help us to taste and see that the Lord is good. Please hear this cry of my heart, dear Lord.

Amen.

THANKFULNESS

Thankfulness is feeling or expressing gratitude. Being grateful and saying so is an easy way for a child to recall what thankfulness means.

God's Word gives a clear command in 1 Thessalonians 5:18, "In everything give thanks for this is the will of God in Christ Jesus concerning you."

We have so much for which to be thankful. First and foremost, we will escape eternal punishment if we have accepted Jesus Christ as our Savior. If God, who gives us all things richly to enjoy, gave us what we truly deserve, our ultimate destination would be eternity in hell. All our accumulated good works can never pay the ransom to save us from the slave market of sin. That's why our precious Savior paid our sin debt in full by sacrificing His life on Calvary's cross. We should be thankful that God is rich in mercy. It is by His grace we are saved through faith.

We have abundant life in Christ Jesus our Lord. Do you express your gratitude to a loving Lord on a regular basis? Or are you apt to grumble and complain when you should be counting your blessings? God is the giver of all gifts. Every good and perfect gift is from above. Let that be a point that is mentioned over and over again in your household. Children must see their parents expressing gratitude for the good and perfect gifts God lavishes upon the family. Thanking God for His provision and protection should be a regular part of your family's daily devotional life.

We cannot expect our children to be grateful if we are ungrateful. Developing and exhibiting a thankful spirit will help us and our children have happy and contented lives. An ungrateful person is unpleasant to be around because that individual lives with a sense of entitlement and is in a constant state of disappointment. Entitlement, a toxic belief, can be defined as the feeling that a person or group deserves to be given something. Thankfulness is a grateful attitude for what you have already been given out of the goodness of God's own heart.

A few everyday examples of thankfulness include:
- Saying grace before meals.
- Saying thank you for gifts that are received or any kindnesses that someone extends to you.
- Writing a thank-you note for a gift or the courtesy of someone's time.
- Expressing appreciation for anyone who helps in any way during a crisis.
- Thanking essential workers or members of the military for their service.
- Extending written appreciation to members of the clergy, teachers, coaches, and others deserving of praise.

Some suggestions to foster thankfulness:

- Post the definition of thankfulness in a prominent place. Discuss the meaning of the word and make sure your child can say what thankfulness means.
- Concentrate on expressing thankfulness for BIG and "little" blessings during family prayers.
- Develop a "thankful list" together as a family for the blessings God has provided. Post it in a place where others will see it. Update your list on a regular basis.
- Make a "blessing box." Whenever something good happens to a member of your family, write it down on a piece of paper and put it into a cheerfully decorated box. Your family can read through past blessings at any point in a given year. Reviewing the contents of the "blessing box" is a great thing to do on Thanksgiving Day. A "blessing box" trains children to be thankful, as it is a practical way to "bless the Lord...and forget none of His benefits." The "blessing box" can establish a family tradition and inspire others to count their blessings.
- Read and discuss such verses as: Psalm 26:7, Ephesians 5:20, Luke 17:11-19, 1 Timothy 2:1, Colossians 3:17.
- Write a thank you note to your pastor, your child's teacher(s), the choir director, your family doctor or dentist, your relatives and friends, your parent's caregiver, and anyone who would be encouraged by your expression of gratitude.
- Make Thanksgiving dinner place cards with thank you Scripture verses on them.
- Make a point of saying thank you to supermarket clerks, customer service representatives, toll collectors, or anyone in your sphere of acquaintance who does a job where they may not be thanked on a routine basis.

- Read and memorize poems that espouse gratitude (See Appendix B).
- Use Psalm 136 and rewrite about 10 verses using a form like this: Oh, give thanks to the Lord, for His mercy endures forever. Each verse could list a part of the history of your family.
- Ensure all gifts, large or small, wanted or unwanted, are acknowledged with a "thank you" in some form.
- Learn to say no. Less is more at times. When you're judicious about how much "stuff" children get or how many activities they get to do, that helps to make them grateful for the times you say yes.
- Teach children to value what they have. Make children earn the next "want."
- Let children see the other side of life by getting them involved in serving others and reading about others less fortunate than themselves. That will help them see how blessed they are.

Teaching children to be appreciative and to give thanks with a grateful heart is something that every parent should aspire to do, first and foremost, by example. We must ask ourselves, do the children in our care see someone who is content with what they have? Are we always grumbling and complaining about this or that and going to great lengths to obtain something that really isn't a necessity?

When we are thankful, truly believing that every good and perfect gift comes from above, our joy increases. Happiness and joy are not the same thing. We can be joyful even in the midst of adversity if we are thankful for God's provision and protection through it all. Children can readily see the gratitude that exists in adults' lives, and they will be better able to emulate thankfulness because it has been on full display for them to see.

A Prayer For Help

Thank You, thank You, thank You, Lord, for saving my soul and making me whole. Help me to give thanks with a grateful heart for Your blessings, great and small. I don't want to take anything for granted. Let my children clearly hear in my words and see in my actions that I value what You have done and are doing for me and our family.

In Jesus' name. Amen.

SELF-CONTROL

Self-control is exercising power over one's actions or feelings. A child can be told that self-control is the ability to do or not do something, even when I want to do something else.

Evidence of self-control, or self-discipline, in a person's life is seen when that individual says the right words and uses the right actions, even when it is uncomfortable to do so, or it is when it is much easier to give into the temptation to do something else.

Here are a few examples of self-control:
- Bypassing all sweet treats to comply with the doctor's orders.
- Limiting time spent on social media.
- The driver who refrains from hoisting up his middle finger or yelling obscenities at the driver who pulls into the spot he's been waiting for.
- Not fighting back and risking suspension when a bully throws the first punch.
- Getting up to maintain the morning regimen of prayer and Bible reading, even when tempted to sleep in.

- Not cursing or trading insults with someone when they have insulted you.
- Not overreacting when your child's teacher has not returned emails, calls, or texts.
- Doing all chores and homework first instead of pursuing other preferred activities.
- Reining in holiday spending and limiting impulse buying at other times during the year.
- Restraining oneself from scrolling through emails or texting during the church service.
- Paying close attention to the person who's talking instead of multitasking, talking over them, or interrupting them.

A quote by Aristotle is, "We are what we repeatedly do...excellence, therefore, isn't just an act but a habit, and life isn't just a series of events, but an ongoing process of self-definition."[8] Thoughtful parents cannot wish their children into the excellent results that only come from hard work, determination, and self-discipline. They must cultivate a home environment that fosters self-control on a daily basis. Schedules and routines are especially helpful for children. Predictability enables them to carry on independently as time goes on without constant monitoring because they know what they're supposed to be doing. Children recognize after a while that it is better to get done what they need to do first so they can have more time left to do what they want to do.

Suggestions to develop self-control include:
- Review and discuss the definition of self-control. Ensure your child can define self-control in her or his own words.
- Discuss why it's necessary to exhibit self-control and have self-discipline.
- Point out everyday examples of self-control and lack of self-control among children and adults.

- Highlight the consequences that occur when children or adults lack self-control.
- Read and discuss such Bible verses as Galatians 5:22-25, Proverbs 25:28, Proverbs 14:17,29, Proverbs 15:1,18, Proverbs 16:32, Romans 12:19, James 1:19, 20.
- Read, discuss, and possibly act out Scripture passages such as James 3:2-10 (control of the tongue), 1 Samuel 24:1-15 (David shows self-control), 1 Samuel 25:2-30 (Abigail helps David use self-control).
- Read books and watch movies where characters display self-control or lack of it. Discuss the outcomes of their behavior.
- Teach children the benefits of deep breathing and removing themselves from tempting situations.
- Read, recite, or memorize poetry that highlights self-control (See Appendix B).
- Model self-control in various areas of your life. Pray for help, if necessary. Enlist the help of an accountability partner.

If you are one of the people who has asked yourself on far too many occasions, "Why did I let those words tumble out of my mouth? Why didn't I just keep my mouth shut?" Or maybe as you looked down at the scale, you wondered, "How in the world did I allow myself to gain so much weight in such a short span of time?" Perhaps, as you recall how a recent fender bender occurred, you want to kick yourself. You know that if you were just content to ride slowly behind the car in front of you instead of impulsively darting into another lane without signaling, the accident would not have happened. Of course, there are countless examples of a lack of self-control in our daily lives that we can consider and use as the impetus to help us get a grip on doing better in this crucial area. When we know better, we should do better because this is what benefits us, our children, and the people we interact with. We can think we have self-control, but that is not enough; we must operate with intentionality. It's worth it because God's blessings abound when we exercise self-control.

A Prayer For Help

Dear God, Jesus is an example of incredible self-control. Please help me to follow in His footsteps in this area when I lack self-control. Help me use wisdom in tempting situations. I need to see clearly what to do and not do. Help me rely on the power of the Holy Spirit so I can engage in the right course of action and restrain myself from engaging in the wrong actions. Keep me accountable, Lord.

In Jesus' name. Amen.

TENDERHEARTEDNESS

Tenderheartedness is being easily moved, as by pity or sorrow, being kind and sympathetic. A tenderhearted person is strong enough to feel the hurts and joys of others. You can tell a child that a tenderhearted person is on the lookout for how someone else might be feeling and cares enough to help that person feel better.

Ephesians 4:32 expresses what tenderheartedness entails in the familiar words, "And be ye kind to one another, tenderhearted, forgiving one another, even as God, for Christ's sake, has forgiven you." The Amplified Bible translation uses the words "compassionate," "understanding," and "loving-hearted" to explain tenderhearted.

As Christ interacted with people, He exhibited the character quality of tenderheartedness on many occasions. The way Jesus treated the lame, the blind, the lepers, and the woman caught in adultery reveals His tender heart towards sinners and people suffering from various afflictions. The parables Jesus told about the Good Samaritan (Luke 10:30-37), the healing of the ten lepers (Luke 17:11-19), and the Prodigal Son (Luke 15:11-32) are dramatic stories that challenge us to be tenderhearted.

The following excerpt from the widely read devotional, *Our Daily Bread*, appeared on October 22, 2021, and captures tenderheartedness as the entry depicts the actions of ten-year-old Chelsea. This little girl received an elaborate art set and discovered that God used art to help her feel better when she was sad. Chelsea then found out that some kids don't have art supplies readily available, and she had an idea to help them. When it was time for her birthday, she asked her friends not to give her gifts for her party, but instead, she invited them to donate art supplies and help fill boxes for children in need. As time went on and with her family's help, this determined and tenderhearted little girl started Chelsea's Charity, an organization that donates art supplies all over the country.[9] Share stories like this one with your children to help them develop tenderheartedness.

Other instances where tenderheartedness is on display include:
- A child shares her lunch with a friend when she notices she doesn't have much to eat.
- A teen carries the grocery packages of his elderly neighbor into her house for her.
- An athlete trips and falls, and his competitor extends a helping hand to get him back on his feet.
- A grocery shopper comes up short, and the next person in line pays the difference so the shopper can leave the store with all his groceries.
- A motorist stops to fix a flat tire for a stranded motorist
- A whiz in math class offers to help another student who has been struggling for weeks.

- A middle school-age child uses the money he's saved to buy Christmas toys for children in the cancer ward of his neighborhood hospital.

Suggestions to foster tenderheartedness include:
- Post and review the definition of tenderheartedness. Make sure your child can tell you in her or his own words what it means to be tenderhearted.
- Display pictures of people engaged in acts of compassion
- Study together the familiar Bible stories of the prodigal son and the Good Samaritan (Bible references were cited previously). Discuss who was tenderhearted and who was not.
- Have a family conversation about what it means to be happy, sad, angry, surprised, worried, and frustrated. Give examples of people who may be experiencing these emotions. Ask your children how someone could be of help to people in those particular situations.
- Identify characters' feelings in stories you read or TV programs you watch as a family. Ask your child if there are ways to help someone experiencing those feelings, if the film or book is lacking in concrete or relevant examples.
- Use puppets with young children to demonstrate tenderhearted actions.
- Role-play the feelings of someone who is ill or suffering from some sort of physical challenge, as well as the appropriate actions that demonstrate tenderheartedness
- Plan and carry out a family project to help someone feel better.
- Plan and carry out a week of "secret helper" projects within your family, for an elderly neighbor, or sick friend.
- Send a special package to someone on the mission field to help combat their feelings of loneliness or isolation.

- Explore poetry that presents a tenderheartedness theme. (See Appendix B).

Anyone who regularly consumes the news can feel despondent about the examples of mean-spirited and horrific acts that dominate the headlines. It's always a breath of fresh air when a good Samaritan story is reported rather than the typical feature stories. On any given day, we'll see and hear more about people taking advantage of other people's misfortunes rather than being swept off our feet by the kindness and compassion extended to others in need. As Christians, our goal should be to bless the "least of these" in our midst. Children tend to be far more charitable than many adults. They're the ones who want to put some coins in the homeless person's cup, bring home the stray cat, or have an already cash-strapped parent buy an extra gift for an underprivileged child. We must nurture their tender hearts and not discourage or chide them when they're looking out for the needs of others.

Whether what we do ever makes the nightly news, let us strive to be like the Good Samaritan and teach our children to do likewise.

A Prayer For Help

Gracious Lord, I acknowledge your kind consideration of me. I could never thank you enough for all the times I received help from You. Jesus, you are my sympathetic High Priest, the One who is always aware of my needs and ready to help me. Please open my eyes to see the needs of others. Open my heart to be willing to help others when their needs come to my attention. May my good example rub off on my children.

Amen

ORDERLINESS

Orderliness can be described as neatness, having everything in its place. Consider orderliness as preparing oneself and one's surroundings so that the greatest efficiency can be achieved. Tell a young child that orderliness means a place for everything and everything in its place.

We see chaos, confusion, and disorder of every sort each day of our lives. But God is not the author of confusion. Everything the Lord has done, is doing, and will do is orderly.

God clearly commands in His word, "Let all things be done decently and in order." (1 Cor. 14:40). Since confusion and disorder are rebellion against what God commands, and we are so prone to operate in this way, parents and other influential adults must work to build orderliness into children's lives.

Children should be taught from a very early age that belongings are kept in specific places; rooms are kept clean, tasks are completed, schedules are followed, etc.

A few examples of orderliness include:
- An oversized wall calendar with color-coded listings to delineate various schedule obligations.
- Crates, plastic containers of various sizes to sort and store objects.
- Classroom cubby spaces to organize children's belongings.
- Specific places where frequently used or emergency objects are located at all times and readily available when needed.
- Children file up to the classroom door by rows to exit the room.
- Parents queue up in the parking lot to drop off or pick up students.

Some suggestions to encourage orderliness are:

- Post and review the definition of orderliness. Display a visual of a neat and tidy space. Make sure your child can tell you in her or his own words what it means to be orderly and well-organized.

- Ask yourself if you are providing a godly example in the way you are "ordering" your life.

- Read and discuss such stories as Jesus feeding the 500 (Mark 6:32-44), Nehemiah directing the rebuilding of the wall of Jerusalem (Nehemiah 2:11-6:15), Joseph organizing the storage of grain for the years of famine (Genesis 41), and Noah building and filling the ark (Gen. 6:13-7:16). Ask your child, "What can we learn about orderliness from this story?"

- Compile work lists with your children that include homework and household chores. Have the children mark off the items as they are completed.

- DO NOT clean up after your children. Even young children can clean up after themselves (it takes patience on your part). You can also try creative ways to make the task more enjoyable, for example, playing music, making a clean-up game, etc. Provide incentives for cleaning up thoroughly in less time.

- Plan and carry out a family "clean up" project. Perhaps some areas in or outside your home, like the garage, storage shed, or laundry room, can benefit from better order.

- Read stories where the advantages of orderliness and/or the disadvantages of disorderliness are clearly seen. Have a discussion and make an application to your life.

- Use music or poetry with the message theme to inspire orderliness. (See Appendix B).

People's lives are so frenetic these days, and sad to say, children are swept up in the frenzy from a young age. Parents who are unable to say NO allow their children's sporting competitions, play dates, recitals, whimsical requests, and the like to be the impetus for far too many family activities, which foster chaotic lifestyles. When family members are like ships passing in the night, ships that never seem to dock at a common time for dinner, family devotions, a weekly church service, a game night, or any joint activity, something is wrong. Over-scheduling and excessive busyness are huge issues for many a 21st-century family. Don't let that be the case for your family. Getting organized and then doing everything in moderation is always sound advice worth considering and implementing in your life.

A Prayer For Help

Dear God, I know I am disorganized. I feel like our lives are spinning out of control. It's as if we're ever running but never winning the race. I am overwhelmed by all this activity, and half the time, I don't even think we're engaged in the right activities. Put wise people in my path who can help me. Help me identify any other useful resources that will get me on the path to having a life where all things are done decently and in order.

In Jesus' name. Amen.

PURITY

Purity can be considered cleanness, innocence, careful correctness, and freedom from foreign or inappropriate elements. You can tell a child that purity means staying away from people, places, or things that don't please God and that pull us away from Him.

The concept of moral purity is very much out of step in today's world. However, God expects every Christian to live a holy life. To be holy is to be morally blameless. God's command for moral excellence is clearly stated in 1 Peter 1:15,16, "But as he who called you is holy, you also be holy in all your conduct, because it is written: 'Be holy, for I am holy.'" Immorality and impurity grieve the heart of a holy God. To live a morally impure life is contrary to God's will for the Christian. It says in 1 Thessalonians 4:7 (CEV), "God didn't choose you to be filthy, but to be pure." Saying NO to ungodliness and worldly passion is very difficult. But the indwelling Holy Spirit is our enabler. Parents and other influential adults must answer the call to moral purity if they expect children to do likewise.

A few examples of purity include:
- Refraining from viewing pornographic photos and films.
- Not listening to music with profane lyrics.
- Avoiding conversations laced with curse words.
- Not telling obscene jokes.
- Avoiding adulterous relationships.
- Not engaging in sex outside of marriage.

Suggestions to foster purity:
- Post an age-appropriate definition of moral purity. Ensure your child can explain the definition in her or his own words.
- Praise God by acknowledging His holiness.
- Read together and memorize the following verses: Isaiah 6:3, Revelation 4:8, Exodus 15:11, Psalm 89:18, Isaiah 43:15, 1 Peter 1:15,16, Leviticus 19:2, Isaiah 57:15, Isaiah 40:25.
- Consider and study together the holiness of Christ. See the following verses: Hebrews 4:15, 1 Peter 2:22, 2 Corinthians 5:21, 1 John 3:5.

- Show your children how Jesus countered the temptations of the devil in Matthew 4:1-11.
- Pursue holiness-scrutinize all your activities and the ones you allow your children to participate in. Ask these questions: "Does this activity violate God's Word?" "Does this activity bring honor to God?" "Would Jesus think this activity is OK?"
- Purge your home of impure music, magazines and books, videos, and posters.
- Replace objectionable activities and materials with God-honoring substitutes like praise music, movies focused on faith themes, and godly poetry that exalts the Lord's holiness (See Appendix B).

Holiness or adhering to a high standard of moral purity is very hard to attain, as fashion, movies, TV shows, social media posts, stand-up comedy, artwork, and the like seem to be pushing the envelope and becoming more and more risqué. Some fashions for girls are quite provocative. Contemporary prom dresses will make the average woman who came of age in the 1950s and 1960s blush as red as a stoplight. It's as if good judgment for what is age-appropriate or proper for a given setting has gone out the window. Christians should be unabashed standard bearers when it comes to modesty. We need not be dowdy when it comes to apparel or so priggish in our demeanor that people wonder if we have any fashion sense or good sense. Clear-cut boundaries in the area of purity will keep us from sliding down the slippery slope of immoral behavior. Listen to your inner voice when you ask if Jesus would be pleased with what is worn, what is seen, or what is done. If the answer is clearly no, make changes that will bring glory and honor to God. Your children will be watching you and other influencers, so see to it that your example of holiness is the one they are inspired to emulate.

A Prayer For Help

Precious Lord, we should be holy as You are holy. Help our family to be pure in ways that please You. Help us stay away from things that violate Your Word. Help us gravitate toward activities that are good and righteous.

Amen.

FORGIVENESS

Forgiveness is giving up the wish to punish or get even with someone who has committed an offense against you. It is the act of pardoning. A definition of forgiveness for a child could be to excuse someone who has hurt you and try not to hurt them for what they did to you.

Paul Boese wisely said, "Forgiveness does not change the past, but it does enlarge the future."[10] Many troubles in our families, churches, and communities stem from wrongs and hurts that have not been forgiven, thus greatly narrowing the possibilities for joy and peace when healing occurs. Learning how to forgive and seek forgiveness can protect us and our children from the torment of resentment, guilt, rage, bitterness, and disappointment. The Lord Jesus, our sinless Savior, set the standard for forgiveness when He cried out from the cross, "Father, forgive these people! They don't know what they are doing." Luke 23:34 (CEV). Jesus lets us know that we must forgive to be forgiven. He clearly states in Luke 6:37, "Judge not, and you shall not be judged. Condemn not, and you shall not be condemned. Forgive, and you will be forgiven."

Daily examples of acts that require forgiveness pale in comparison to the sins our Lord forgave while dying on the cross, but some common situations include:

- Lying about something
- Stealing
- Ruining someone's possessions
- Gossiping
- Deceiving or cheating someone
- Slandering another person
- Losing one's temper
- Abusing or neglecting someone
- Failing to meet responsibilities or obligations
- Committing adultery

To teach forgiveness, we must recognize the importance of being a forgiving person. The best way to learn how to forgive is to see how God forgives us. Forgiveness comes as a result of confession. Confession means acknowledging our sin without excuses or conditions. When we seek forgiveness, we should "own up" to our wrongs clearly and plainly. God promises in 1 John 1:9, "If we confess our sins, He is faithful and just to forgive us our sins and cleanse us from all unrighteousness." Forgiveness is the basis for restored fellowship. God says, "I have blotted out, as a thick cloud, your transgressions and, like a cloud, your sins. Return to Me, for I have redeemed you." Isaiah 44:22. Once sin is forgiven, it's best not to bring the matter up again. This is how God deals with us: "Their sins and their lawless deeds I will remember no more." Hebrews 10:17

So, how do we teach children to forgive others and seek forgiveness when they have wronged someone? We teach by our example. We should be quick to acknowledge any way we may have wronged our children or others. When someone comes seeking forgiveness, we should readily grant it without harping on the fact that they committed an offense against us. Forgiveness is the basis for blessing in life. Psalm 32 reflects the state of contentment that results from sins that are forgiven. Forgiveness replaces a perpetual state of agitation, resentment, rage, or bitterness over previous wrongs with the joy of the Lord.

Suggestions to teach forgiveness:
- Post the definition in a prominent place. Ensure your child grasps the definition and can provide age-appropriate examples of forgiveness.
- Point out how forgiving God is. Share the verses mentioned in this section with your children.
- Read about the life of Joseph. Discuss whom he forgave and how he showed he didn't hold on to the offenses his brothers committed against him.
- Point out acts of forgiveness exhibited among your family members, people in your community, and by characters in literature or films.
- If your children appear to be hurting over something, get to the bottom of the problem. Do whatever you can to help them forgive the person that offended them.
- Praise acts of forgiveness.
- Read, recite, or memorize poems that shed light on the act of forgiveness. (See Appendix B).

Countless families have heartbreaking sagas about members who refuse to forgive someone over something that resulted in a great offense, deep hurt, or unimaginable hardship. Years may go by without the feuding parties speaking on the phone, attending family gatherings, or acknowledging special occasions. The chasm grows deeper and wider, and innumerable people suffer because of the unresolved issues. Seldom is it just the individuals involved who refuse to forgive one another. The more heinous the act or acts that were committed against a person or that individual's loved one, the harder it is to forgive the perpetrator.

Lack of forgiveness can be a toxic force in the life of the person who refuses to forgive. Not one of us is perfect; we've all sinned and come short of the glory of God.

Where would any of us be if God marked every one of our iniquities and refused to forgive us of our sins and cleanse us from all unrighteousness? As we look to Christ's stellar example of forgiveness and rely on the Holy Spirit's power, we can forgive others as Christ Jesus has forgiven us.

A Prayer For Help

Dear Lord, I am reminded of Your words on the cross, "Father, forgive them; they know not what they do." Help me to be humble enough to ask for forgiveness. May I be strong enough to grant forgiveness to the people who have truly hurt me. I sincerely want to be better equipped to teach my children lessons about forgiveness that I have learned myself.

In Jesus' name. Amen.

It's an indisputable fact that it takes time and dedication to develop character in children. Don't slack off because you are tired, frustrated, confused, angry, or your friends raising children don't see the importance of character development. You are the most important role model your children have.

With a parent's words and deeds, they instill the character that shapes their children's lives, and when godly traits are taught, that evolves into the character that results in a good name. In Proverbs 22:1[a] it states, "A good name is to be chosen rather than great riches." I was struck by the weighty words that Johnnie Bettis uttered to his son Jerome as he left for college, "Son, I don't have much to give you. But I do have a good name, so don't mess it up."[11] Jerome quoted his father years later in his American Professional Football Hall of Fame acceptance speech.

I've heard it said that you can work diligently at forging a good reputation for 30 years, only to ruin it in 30 seconds by engaging in some regrettable act. A perfect example is the predicament actor Will Smith found himself in after slapping 2022 Academy Awards host Chris Rock, who made a joke about Jada Pinkett Smith's hair. It appeared that Smith's wife, who suffers from alopecia, didn't take too kindly to what was said. There certainly were wiser courses of action that Will Smith could have taken instead of slowly walking onto the stage and slapping Chris Rock in front of millions of viewers. About 30 minutes later, he won the Oscar for his role in King Richard, where he portrayed the famous father of tennis stars Venus and Serena Williams. The fallout from the slap, dubbed the slap heard around the world, greatly overshadowed the praise Smith rightfully deserved for a stellar portrayal of Richard Williams. Will Smith was quite fortunate that Chris Rock, who did not retaliate in any way, took the moral high road and declined to press charges for assaulting him. Days after the debacle, Will Smith resigned from the Motion Picture Arts Academy in disgrace. Shortly thereafter, the Academy's board of governors voted to ban Smith from attending the annual Oscars Ceremony or any other Academy function for the next decade. That incident will be a permanent blemish on Will Smith's character, probably resulting in many more unforeseen consequences stemming from that one impulsive action. Choices, both good and bad, are the result of the character that we possess. All choices have consequences; a fact we must teach our children from an early age.

We all do regrettable things for which we need to apologize or make right in some specific way. No one is perfect except our Savior. Exemplifying good character is a choice. As Heraclitus stated, "The content of your character is your choice. Day by day, what you choose, what you think, and what you do is who you become."[12] Parents exhibiting excellent character and making godly choices make it easier for their children to follow in their footsteps. Your home is the best place to continually make good choices that build the habits that translate into excellent character. Make that your mission.

Character is the Key presents twelve character qualities:
- Obedience
- Reverence
- Wisdom
- Faith
- Honesty
- Patience
- Thankfulness
- Self-Control
- Tenderheartedness
- Orderliness
- Purity
- Forgiveness

With twelve months in a year, you can feature or focus on one quality per month while also working on other qualities at any given time. Of course, there are many more character qualities that can be inculcated into a child's life: resilience, humility, courage, perseverance, joyfulness, contentment, diligence, love, and commitment, to name a few. This chapter sought to provide a template for character development. The elements presented here are designed to provide tools to develop godly character traits in the lives of children. Remember, godly character is the key to unlocking many blessings for your children as they journey through life. Character is the key.

SIX

Biblical Behavior Modification

Behavior modification is the process of changing behavior or regulating actions. I have entitled this section of *A Blueprint for Building Children: Following God's Plan,* Biblical Behavior Modification, as I will present methods that rely on God's ways and means to bring about change. I believe Biblical behavior modification is a careful, thoughtful process applied by conscientious Christian parents. It demands knowledge, dedication, prayerful persistence, and continued reinforcement to bring about God's righteous results.

God's ways and man's ways are vastly different. Christian parents are constantly bombarded with anti-biblical messages as it relates to parenting. Many parents have abandoned God's thinking for views expressed on social media, in magazines, in child psychology books, on TV talk, or in reality shows. Don't misunderstand me, excellent parenting advice can come from a variety of sources; however, if the advice is diametrically opposed to what is presented in the Word of God, then Christian parents should be very wary. Never forget that God is the Source, and everyone and everything else is a resource. The blueprint for building secure, capable, joyful children is found in the Bible.

The deepest desire of Christian parents should be that their children come to saving faith in Jesus Christ. Their hope should be that they grow up becoming image bearers of the Savior who can help them navigate this wicked world, making a difference in His precious name. As parents and other concerned adults adopt the Lord's ways, we'll see His promises fulfilled in our lives and the lives of our children. God provides all we need to see the enormously challenging job of child-rearing through to completion.

Biblical behavior modification targets the inner attitudes of the heart. Contemporary approaches focus on outward behavior. This chapter presents several God approved/ordained methods, and each one has a particular role in the child-rearing process. These five methods include:

1. Prayer
2. Instruction
3. Encouragement
4. Correction
5. Counseling

PRAYER

Prayer is divine communion with our heavenly Father. In *The Hour That Changes the World,* Dick Eastman writes, "Prayer is the vision of the believer. It gives eyes to our faith. In prayer, we see beyond ourselves and focus spiritual eyes on God's infinite power."[1] This quote may sound a bit lofty and make you feel as if prayer is an elusive activity, something you can't really get a handle on because, after all, God is high and lifted up. He is far exalted in rank, dignity, eminence, and character above each and every one of us. Nevertheless, the Lord is very approachable in prayer. We don't need fancy words or long, stilted, or formal prayers. We simply need to boldly approach God's throne of grace, believing

He hears and answers our prayers. Take Hebrews 4:16 (NIV) to heart. It says, "Let us then approach God's throne of grace with confidence so that we may receive mercy and find grace to help us in our time of need."

As parents or other adults concerned about children, we would do well to pray with and for children, for our own children, for our friends' children, and for all the children of the world. Our earnest pleadings before the Lord have a profound effect. If we look at our Savior's life, we constantly find Jesus praying. Where there is frequency, consistency, and intensity of prayer, there is a display of God's power. More than likely, you've heard the expression, "Prayer changes things." At the end of the day, we're the ones who need changing. Adults and children must be changed to what God wants us to be.

1 Thessalonians 5:17 instructs us to "Pray without ceasing." Ceaseless prayers concerning our children will not go unanswered. James 5:16 (NIV) states, "Therefore, confess your sins to each other and pray for each other so that you may be healed. The prayer of a righteous person is powerful and effective." I've heard many a well-meaning Christian rattle off that verse from memory, but do many Christians really believe their prayers make a difference? If so, why do many Christians forfeit the opportunities they have to pray? We put forth a bunch of excuses like, I'm too tired or too busy to pray. Jesus was very busy during the three years of His personal ministry, and there are numerous indications in the Scriptures that He was tired and weary. However, in Matthew, Mark, Luke, and John, we see Jesus praying continually. I've heard folks complain that they don't know what to say. In the Psalms and other books of the Bible, we find all sorts of prayers about every conceivable thing. Pray God's Word to Him with righteous intent, truly desiring His perfect will in a matter, and you can be sure He'll answer you. God's Word never returns void; it prospers in the thing to which it is sent. Understand this; however, the answers to your prayers may not come at the time you

want but delayed does not mean denied. Your requested answer may arrive, but not by way of circumstances you would have preferred. It may also be the case that the answer to your prayers is not what you asked for. Trust that God truly knows best.

Let me share a personal anecdote about the power of prayer and how it factored into a life-altering event that occurred thirteen years after I gave my life to the Lord. The incident spotlights how God was faithful to answer my prayers and the prayers of others on behalf of my unsaved husband.

It was June 30, 1995, an absolutely gorgeous day that began with me being outside on our deck for morning devotions. Our young son, not quite two years old at the time, was sleeping peacefully. I was in our hot tub, looking up at an azure blue sky. Tears streamed down my face while I mulled over the events of recent weeks and wondered what it would take for my husband to come to the Lord. Years and years had passed since the Mother's Prayer Group that I had initiated started praying for Quinn's salvation. We gathered once a month not only to pray for our children's concerns in particular, but family matters in general. My husband remained rather stubborn and hard-hearted about a relationship with the Lord, even though he knew people were truly concerned for his soul. About the middle of May, my husband was involved in a multiple-car accident, and he smugly told me to tell the ladies in the Mother's Prayer Group thanks for their travel mercy prayers. Although to hear Quinn relate the details of the accident, he walked away without serious injury because of his stellar driving skills. Those of us who prayed for him regularly knew that God was trying to get his attention. But Quinn would have none of it. He felt comfortable being a chanting Buddhist, and on more than one occasion, he told me flat-out that I'd become a Buddhist before he became a Christian. So it was on June 30, 1995, just a few weeks after the car accident, that God moved powerfully to let us know that He was in charge and He had other plans for Quinn's life.

Around 6:30 p.m. on the evening of June 30th, I was rushing to finish my workout. I knew Quinn would soon be arriving home after his weekly racquetball game. He always played with his best friend Jake, someone who'd go to the ends of the earth and back to do what was needed to help Quinn. These two guys had a decades-long faithful friendship that few people experience.

The phone rang at about 6:50 p.m. Though I could tell that Jake was trying to sound calm, there was a certain tension in his voice when he said, "I'm coming to pick you up because Quinn's on his way to St. Peter's Hospital." Of course, my heart fell to my feet. By the time I grabbed my son's stroller and something for him to eat, along with making calls to a few of the prayer warriors, Jake was at my house. I still had my workout clothes on and a towel around my neck when we got in the car. The first thing I noticed was that Jake was headed toward Robert Wood Johnson University Hospital and not St. Peter's. He admitted to being so nervous when he called me that he told me the name of the wrong hospital. As soon as I made my way to the ER, I found the doctor who was examining Quinn's chest X-ray. He informed me about the large clot, and the fact that Quinn had a massive heart attack. They were going to administer a clot-busting drug called TPA, which had the very rare side effect of causing the heart to beat wildly out of control. When I laid eyes on Quinn, I could see he was in excruciating pain. He asked for the towel around my neck, a remnant from my workout, to prop up his head.

I tried to be as encouraging as possible, letting him know that as soon as I could reach her, I would drop our son back home so his sister, Aliya, who was on break from college, could keep an eye on him. Jake and I would come back and wait it out until he was admitted to a room.

I rushed back to the waiting room to find little Quinn and "Uncle" Jake doing just fine. I told Jake that Quinn had a heart attack, but things seemed quiet at the moment. To my mind, things were going as well as could be expected. I informed Jake about the plan and said I'd return as soon as it was okay to leave. I told him, I'm sure I'll be right back. That was just before 9:00 p.m.

Quinn received TPA, and initially, everything was going okay. I glanced at the patient monitoring equipment to check out Quinn's vital signs. Because I had just recently done some consulting work for two manufacturers of patient monitoring equipment, work requiring quite a bit of research and preparation for the assignments, I actually knew what I was looking at. I felt comfortable with the steady heartbeat and good blood pressure numbers. Then, like a lightning flash at about 9:15 p.m., Quinn's heart started beating erratically, and his blood pressure plunged. I could see and hear on the monitor that he was in trouble, and I knew the medical team was going to kick me out of the area. Sure enough, I was told to leave.

What ensued was like a scene from one of the medical TV shows. I experienced some of the most harrowing moments of my life. Someone came running down the hall with a defibrillator. Since I wasn't seated that far away from the chaos, the drawn curtain didn't prevent me from hearing what was going on. I distinctly heard the sound of Quinn's heart flat-lining. I glanced at the clock and noted it was now 9:20 p.m.

Of course, I was praying all the while the team was frantically working on my husband. I took great comfort in knowing other people were praying for Quinn, too. I wanted the Lord to spare my husband's life for obvious reasons, but I was also concerned that if he didn't survive, hell would be his destination. I voiced my confidence to God that little Quinn and I would be all right because of God's faithfulness. No matter what, I wanted God's will to be done. The first three attempts to revive Quinn, lasting about 10 minutes from the start of the episode, proved unsuccessful. And then, miraculously, at 9:32 p.m., after a rare fourth attempt of the high voltage defibrillator pads shocking Quinn, I heard my husband utter an expletive. I exclaimed, "Thank You, Jesus!" Little did I know at that time that Quinn had an out-of-body experience during those fateful 12 minutes. Time seemed to be whizzing by. What must Jake be thinking? Of course, he'd be suspicious that something had gone wrong. My husband wasn't wheeled out into the hall, awaiting transport to the ICU, until close to midnight. He looked horrible. His color was an ashen gray. There were burn marks down the side of his body from the places the defibrillator pads connected with his skin. I could tell he was in excruciating pain again, more so than earlier in the evening. I had to hold back the tears and be strong. Quinn's first words to me were, "Well, I guess... I've been saved for a reason."

Jake, little Quinn, and I were finally reunited in the corridor leading to Quinn's ICU room at about 12:30 a.m. I was shocked to see our little toddler boy pushing his own stroller. Both Jake and I were amazed because he was singing in his sweet little voice, "God is So Good." I told my son, "One day, you'll know just how good God is."

I hope my personal anecdote helped you see why I'm such an advocate for a faithful and fervent prayer life. In the previously cited situation, I was helpless. All I could do was pray.

Of course, there are countless books about prayer that you can read to assist you as you cultivate your unique prayer life. My copy of *Prayers That Avail Much*, given to me in the early 1980s, is highlighted and battered and tear-stained. It was the springboard to an ever-increasing and intensifying prayer life that continues to this day. I also highly recommend Dick Eastman's book, which I quoted at the beginning of this section. Eastman carves an hour timeframe into the following twelve prayer components: Praise, Waiting, Confession, Scripture Praying, Watching, Intercession, Petition, Thanksgiving, Singing, Meditation, Listening, and Praise.[2] You may be wondering what watching or waiting is all about. Perhaps you're not sure about the distinction between intercession and petition. Eastman defines these terms and provides excellent examples for clarification, Scriptural references for review, and a step-by-step approach to integrate a particular prayer component into your personal prayer life. Of course, it's very beneficial to educate yourself about prayer. Reading books on the subject will prove helpful, but nothing, absolutely nothing, takes the place of earnest pleadings before God. You must pray! It isn't rocket science; if you want God to move in your situation, PRAY!

Examine your heart and be brutally honest. Ask yourself these questions:

- How much time do I spend on screens (not counting work-related screen time)?
- How does this amount of time compare with the time I spend praying with and for my children?
- How much time do I spend yelling at or lecturing my children?
- Does my prayer time with and for my children even come close to the previously cited expenditures of time?

It's a simple rule of thumb: if you want to get a glimpse of what's important to you, look at where you allocate your time and how long you engage in a given activity. Do your children ever catch you praying? Would it be more likely they'd catch you arguing with or gossiping about someone rather than hear you praying earnestly for that same person?

An authentic prayer life requires you to act. Get into the habit of praying early and often about the things that concern you. One of the best pieces of advice I ever received was, "Say less, pray more." I often remind myself, "Stephanie, less say, more pray!" Set your alarm, get out of bed, and pray. Before you lay your head down at night, pray. During the day, take time to pray. Pray before meals. Pray spontaneously if something perplexing arises or you're troubled and anxious about something. Pray when danger arises. Pray about people, projects, problems, places, and opportunities. Pray about anything and everything. And by all means, encourage your children to pray, too. Don't be afraid that your children will get bored when they pray or be disappointed if God doesn't answer their prayers in the exact way they want them answered. That's where parental instruction comes in. You'll be their guide through the process. There are numerous children's prayer books available, many with lovely illustrations, to get your children started on their own faith journey. It's never too soon to help a little child realize that prayer is a special time we spend talking to God. A little one can be asked to bow her head and fold her hands. A parent can encourage a young child to say amen at the end of a short prayer (the marathon prayers are best left for your time alone with God). Once your child can verbally express himself to you, encourage him to "talk" to God, but never force the child to pray.

Yes, pray without ceasing! Think of prayer as one of the best habits you can cultivate for yourself and help promote for your children. It's a spiritual discipline that's worth every bit of effort and energy that you'll ever expend engaging in it. Prayer will be the best eternal investment you can make on behalf of your children. Heartfelt and decisive prayers will reap incalculable dividends in their lives.

The Parent's Prayer that follows was handed to me at the end of one of the *Blueprint* workshops that I conducted decades ago. The participant simply stated, "I found this and thought you might be interested in it, and maybe you can share it with others." The Parent's Prayer, author unknown, has so many elements that touched my heart back then. I can recall praying this prayer faithfully and fervently, and it accomplished much in my life and in the lives of my own children and those whom I influenced down through the years.

The Parent's Prayer

O Heavenly Father, make me a better parent. Teach me to understand my children, to listen patiently to what they have to say, and to answer all their questions kindly. Keep me from interrupting them or contradicting them. Make me as courteous to them as I would have them be to me. Forbid that I should ever laugh at their mistakes or resort to shame or ridicule when they displease me. May I never punish them for my own selfish satisfaction or to show my power. Let me not tempt my child to lie or steal. And guide me hour by hour that I may demonstrate by all that I say and do that honesty produces happiness. Reduce, I pray, the meanness in me. And when I am out of sorts, help me, O Lord, to hold my tongue. May I ever be mindful that my children are children, and I should not expect of them the judgment of adults. Let me not rob them of the opportunity to wait on themselves and to make decisions. Bless me with the bigness to grant them all their reasonable requests and the courage to deny them privileges I know will do them harm. Make me fair and just and kind. And fit me, O Lord, to be loved and respected and imitated by my children.

SELAH

I hope the word selah caught your attention. How could it not jump off the page when I deliberately bolded the word and used the largest font possible? Perhaps this is a word you're unfamiliar with. Did you go to your smartphone and look up the definition? Or maybe you encountered this word a while ago in the Psalms, noticing it at the end of a sentence, and you looked it up then. In the Amplified version of the Bible, you'll see the word translated as pause and calmly think of that. The psalmist wants you to take a moment to ponder what you just read. The Unger's Bible Dictionary definition of selah is: "Probably a musical notation indicating an intended pause."[3] Dictionary.com states that, "Selah is an expression occurring frequently in the psalms, thought to be a liturgical or musical direction, probably a direction by the leader to raise the voice or perhaps an indication of a pause."[4] By now, I trust you get the idea that I don't want you to rush on to the next section of this chapter. I'd like you to pause and think calmly and seriously about the role prayer plays in your life. Is prayer an integral part of your existence, or is it some afterthought that you resort to after you feel like you've exhausted all other options? Is your prayer life on again or off again, depending on whether the answers to your prayers suit your fancy? Perhaps the question posed in Corrie Ten Boom's quote, "Is prayer your steering wheel or your spare tire?"[5] gets you thinking.

As a parent, you routinely expect your children to do many things they'd prefer to skip, like homework or chores. You may have to do some explaining or cajoling, or other things to get them going in the right direction, but eventually, they see how much they can achieve from putting in the work that they're expected to do. God expects us to pray. It's hard work, but incredible things can be achieved as a result of earnest prayer. I have incorporated a selah moment at the end of this section before you move on to the topic of Instruction. Resist the temptation to hurry into the next section of this chapter. I hope you'll pause and complete the prayer project that appears below. I believe you'll derive great benefits as you engage in the hard work of prayer. In fact, it is my prayer for you to experience transformative results in your family.

Prayer Project

1. Determine where you're going to record your prayer requests and answers to prayers. Some people prefer journal books, while others may want to utilize a tech option. Ease of use and ready access are the most important criteria.

2. Write the date.

3. Make a list of family-oriented concerns. Don't prioritize your concerns at this point.

4. Wait at least one day and then return to your list. Write down any additional concerns that popped into your mind after completing your original list. Write the new date and the top two or three concerns you'd like to focus on for the prayer project. Write your concerns in terms of your desired results. An example might be: My prayer is for my husband not to perish but to believe in Christ's saving work on the cross, so he'll be saved and have eternal life.

5. Using a Bible concordance, search to see if there are any verses that relate to your concern(s). Write out some Scripture(s) that pertain to your concern(s). For example, "For I am not ashamed of the gospel, because it is the power of God that brings salvation to everyone who believes: first to the Jew, then to the Gentile." Romans 1:16 (NIV): "that everyone who believes may have eternal life in him. For God so loved the world that he gave his one and only Son, that

whoever believes in him shall not perish but have eternal life."-John 3:15,16 (NIV) "But these are written that you may believe that Jesus is the Christ, the Son of God and that by believing you may have life in his name." -John 20:31

6. Commit to praying morning, noon, and night for your concerns, utilizing elements of the Scriptures in your prayers. Do this for a period of three weeks. For example: "Lord, right now my husband is far from You, but I am not ashamed of the gospel, and I believe it is the power that brings salvation to everyone who believes. Help soften my husband's hard heart of unbelief. Enable him to see that the Scriptures were written to help him believe that Jesus is the Christ, the Son of God, and that by believing, he might have the abundant life You've promised. Please help my husband to see how much You love him and how much I love him, and how believing in Christ's saving work will enable him to have eternal life. In Jesus' name. Amen."

7. Write down the date and any answers to your prayers that occur during those three weeks.

8. At the end of three weeks, write down the answers to these questions:
    - How did praying morning, noon, and night about my concern(s) draw me closer to God?
    - How did praying morning, noon, and night draw me closer to the person I was praying about and/or change my perspective on the situation?
    - What were the specific answers to my prayers?
    - How can I thank God in word and/or deed for the answers to my prayers?
    - What was the most important "take-away" from completing the prayer project?
    - How should I proceed in prayer from this point?

Just before I directed you to the Prayer Project, I stated that it is my prayer for you to experience transformative results in your family. I truly hope the transformation process accelerated during the past three weeks. Don't stop now. Keep praying, hoping, and trusting. Have faith to believe that God is able to do exceedingly abundantly above anything you could ever envision (Ephesians 3:20). Do you remember my husband, the chanting Buddhist, who had a massive heart attack and out-of-body experience that led to him being saved? About 20 years after his dramatic "Come to Jesus" moment, Quinn and I became the co-founders of the non-profit organization that established New Covenant Christian Academy in Plainfield, NJ. That feat was all the more miraculous because the endeavor started with a mere $250 and a handful of supporters. So, continue to pray without ceasing for everyone and everything, but especially pray with and for your children.

My Ardent Prayer

God of glory and amazing grace, I bring before You every reader of **A Blueprint For Building Children: Following God's Plan** *and every child in their immediate care and circle of influence. You know every need, every concern, and every dream that they have now or will ever have because You're omniscient. The deep and sincere desire of my heart is that You will bless their prayers abundantly, revealing Your unsurpassed power. Not only do I hope they'll see Your omnipotence on full display but let them experience Your unconditional and unfailing love in the process. Because You're omnipresent, it doesn't matter where a reader may be or what they are currently experiencing; You are there. Praise the Lord! Let our hearts be grateful for the transformative results that You will bring about in every reader's family.*

In Jesus' name. Amen and amen!

INSTRUCTION

The core of Biblical Behavior Modification is instruction backed up by parental example. One of the most instructive books of the Bible with practical guidance for daily living is the book of Proverbs.

The major emphasis in the book of Proverbs is the recurring contrast between the wise individual and the fool. Proverbs 1:2-4 (CEV) states, "Proverbs will teach you wisdom and self-control and how to understand sayings with deep meanings. You will learn what is right and honest, and fair. From these, an ordinary person can learn to be smart, and young people can gain knowledge and good sense." I'll pose a rhetorical question: what parent would not like their child to grow up to be prudent, just, and knowledgeable? Of course, that's an admirable goal. Unfortunately, the deepest desires of our hearts regarding our children will not come to fruition without putting in a lot of hard work. Instruction should consist of intentional, careful, diligent teaching carried out by dedicated parents and other concerned adults.

The Bible exhorts adults to "Train up a child in the way he should go, and when he is old, he will not depart from it." Proverbs 22:6. It's not an ironclad promise that your child will never go astray, even when you work diligently in your teaching efforts, because God does not override a person's free will. But you can be sure that children will be more inclined to stay on the road to righteousness when parents do their part in the child-rearing process and enlist the help of a "village" of like-minded individuals to partner with them in their endeavors. Keep in mind that one of the most important yet simple truths you should teach your children is that Jesus loves them. Jesus' love for them and for the whole human race was so profound and personal that He was willing to die on a cruel cross to secure salvation for whoever believes in Him (John 3:16). Leading your children to saving faith in Jesus Christ should be your first priority.

Of course, God wants parents to be diligent when teaching children right from wrong in all areas of life. This is clearly seen in Deuteronomy 6:6-8 in His instructions to the Israelites, "And these words, which I command you today shall be in your heart. You shall teach them diligently to your children, and you shall talk of them when you sit in your house, when you walk by the way, when you lie down, and when you rise up. You shall bind them as a sign on your hand, and they shall be as frontlets between your eyes." Teaching children about God need not always be a formal, regimented occurrence. As we see in the previous passage, instruction is going on in everyday aspects of life. There are teachable moments that parents and other adults can seize readily if their minds are attuned to spiritual matters. I'm a huge advocate for family devotions, relatively short sessions that can occur after a meal, in the car, or while sitting in the backyard or in a park. A basic template is:

- A short prayer.
- A passage of Scripture or a short story.
- A brief discussion about what the Scripture passage or story means to everyone.
- A brief closing prayer.

You'd be surprised by what children absorb from family devotions. It's a wonderful spiritual discipline that you can foster even when your children are young. I adopted family devotions with my daughter as soon as I found out the benefits of the practice, but Aliya was already almost eleven years old. My son was exposed to some sort of family devotions from the time he was a toddler. I was totally stunned one Saturday afternoon when my son Quinn, who was about 12 at the time, asked me to stop to look at a particular tree while we were on a walk along a hiking trail. He asked me to leave the trail and get close to the tree as he pointed out that the hole in the trunk caused him to think the tree was rotting. Quinn went on to tell me that sin was like that in our lives, ruining what was once healthy. You could have knocked me over with a feather. We must never underestimate the power of the Holy Spirit to make a connection with someone, no matter their age.

It can be difficult to carve out the time when schedules are always so busy but make a small commitment of time to do daily family devotions and stick with it. You can gradually make changes in your routine as time passes and needs change. Your peers may think family devotions are impossible to pull off, but don't be discouraged by their negative point of view. Of course, it's hard to rise up and then stay above the fray, but God's grace and the work of the Holy Spirit will enable you to make great strides in this area.

Instruction should transpire on a daily basis. The home is the first and most influential classroom a child ever enters. Godly parents must take their responsibility to instruct their children in the things of the Lord very seriously. Nowadays, I see some Christian parents giving much more thought to whether their children will play sports than whether they'll attend church and Sunday School regularly on Sunday mornings. There are parents who send their children to religious schools and/ or services but do not attend religious services themselves. Their Bibles collect dust, and the family rarely prays together for their own needs or anyone else's concerns. What does that kind of thing say to their children? Children can spot a hypocrite a mile away. Hypocrisy is repugnant to everyone, especially children. Every member of the family can benefit from instruction so that all are rooted, grounded, and established in God's Word.

Here is another passage of Scripture that indicates that God holds parents responsible for instructing their children about Him. Psalm 78:1-7 (ESV) says, "Give ear, O my people, to my teaching; incline your ears to the words of my mouth! I will open my mouth in a parable; I will utter dark sayings from of old, things that we have heard and known, that our fathers have told us. We will not hide them from their children but tell the coming generation the glorious deeds of the Lord, and his might, and the wonders that he has done." Before reading the rest of the passage, I want you to ask yourself, "Do I hide the goodness of the Lord from my children by not praising and thanking God in their presence for all the wonderful things He's done for our family?" The psalmist writes further, "He established a testimony in Jacob, and appointed a law in Israel, which he commanded our fathers to teach their children, that the next generation might know them, the children yet unborn, and arise and tell them to their children, so they should set their hope in God and not forget the works of God, but keep his commandments;" With all the things that are going on around us, it's so easy to sink into hopelessness and despair. That's why we must not forget the works of God. Instruct your children to set their hope in God by teaching them diligently and setting the appropriate example for them in your home.

Here are a number of additional Scripture passages to encourage adults to instruct children about matters pertaining to God:

- Psalm 145:4 "One generation shall praise Your works to another and shall declare Your mighty acts."
- Psalm 34:11 (NIV) "Come, my children, listen to me; I will teach you the fear of the Lord."
- Isaiah 38:19 (NIV) "The living, the living-they praise you, as I am doing today; parents tell their children about your faithfulness."
- Joel 1:3 "Tell it to your children, and let your children tell it to their children, and their children to the next generation."
- Ephesians 6:4 (NIV) "Fathers, do not exasperate your children; instead, bring them up in the training and instruction of the Lord."

The wisdom that is derived from the Word of God is a lamp for our feet and light for our path (Psalm 119:105) to keep us going in the right direction. Availing ourselves of God's wisdom guides us through life and guards us against sin and error that can result in disastrous consequences. Life is definitely a labyrinth, an intricate combination of oftentimes confusing paths from which we must choose, and that's why it's so easy to lose our way. God always knows the best way for us to go, and the more parents know about the Lord and His ways, the easier it is to instruct their children in the way they should go.

Earlier, I mentioned the fact that some Christian parents give more thought to whether their children will play sports than whether they'll attend church services, Sunday School, and/or Christian youth groups. I have an undergraduate degree in Health and Physical Education, and I have competed in an organized sport, so I am well aware of the incredible benefits and valuable life lessons that can be gained from healthy competition and participation in sports. However, sports or other interests should not occupy the preeminent place in our lives or our children's lives. A family's calendar should not totally revolve around practice schedules, tournaments or competitions, auditions, and the like.

Keep God on the throne of your heart where He belongs, and then prayerfully consider how to best prioritize, organize, and concentrate on activities that help develop your children in the areas of body, soul, and spirit. The juggling act is never easy, but God will help you.

I'd like to offer an example from my daughter's life. Aliya was a competitive roller skater (think ice skating, but with the same jumps and spins done on roller skates) from the age of ten to eighteen. She moved through the competitive divisions and finally retired after skating in World Class Ladies, the highest-ranking women's division. At the outset, I was pretty hardcore - no skating on Sunday, period! Aliya showed a lot of potential, and coaches warned me that she'd never get very far in the sport without practicing and competing on Sunday. I had drawn a line of demarcation. Aliya had to be in church, attend Sunday School, and honor the Lord's Day. We were always careful from day one about the music we chose for her routines, the choreography, and the way she was costumed. When Aliya turned fourteen, she was quite active in the church youth group, and the leaders were challenging the young people to use their talents and abilities to serve the Lord and boldly share their Christian testimony. Aliya decided she would no longer skate to secular music. Her first routine after making that bold decision was skated to the hymn, *"What A Friend We Have in Jesus."* After an appeal from my daughter to practice and compete on Sunday because, as she put it, "I'm the only Jesus some of my skating friends will ever see," I relented. Believe me, her boldness in presenting the Gospel through selected choreographic moves and her choice of music created quite a stir. She learned to articulate why she was doing what she was doing. The same year Aliya abandoned secular music in favor of skating to Christian music, she qualified for the Junior Olympics National Championships. She placed third at Nationals, even without the benefit of her coach being there with her at the competition. To this day, there are many life lessons that skating provided for my daughter that have contributed to her personal and professional success. You may be wondering if I abandoned my stance on attending church on Sundays. Actually, I did not; Aliya always had to be in attendance at a morning or evening service, but not both services on days she competed. She made a concerted effort to keep up with Sunday School lessons and youth group activities. And in addition to that, she was enrolled at a Christian school. Whenever she skated at Regional or National events and could not attend our home church, I'd do my research (and there was no internet back then) to find a suitable church near the skating venue so she could attend service. Aliya won her share of medals, trophies, and plaques along the way, but what she did for Christ during that young and impressionable season of her life will last forever. Several of her friends came to know the Lord. We must never put God in a box when it comes to who or what He'll use to teach and reach people.

Are you saying to yourself, I never really considered my parental role as that of a teacher? Perhaps you feel it's hard enough to function as a protector and provider for your children. Think of it this way: nothing is too hard for God. He'll equip you for any and every role you must step into to raise your children. What you must do is instruct your children with intentionality because if you are not teaching your children, someone, or something else will move into your rightful place to fill the void. Chapter Five makes the case for why it's important to instill godly character in children and offers some suggestions about ways to build character. "Character is the Key" presents twelve godly character traits that will help your children navigate the challenges, opportunities, frustrations, perplexities, sorrows, and joys of life. Teach your children how to love in the true meaning of the word. The true meaning of love is depicted in 1 Corinthians 13:4-8a (LB), which states, "Love is very patient and kind, never jealous or envious, never boastful, or proud, never haughty, or selfish or rude. Love does not demand its own way. It is not irritable or touchy. It does not hold grudges and will hardly even notice when others do it wrong. It is never glad about injustice but rejoices whenever truth wins out. If you love someone, you will be loyal to them no matter what the cost. You will always believe in him, always expect the best of him, and always stand your ground defending him. All the special gifts and powers from God will someday come to an end, but love goes on forever." If your children grouse and complain that it's too hard to love and wonder why they must work so hard at being loving, tell them that's what God wants us to do. When the religious leaders challenged Jesus to answer their question about which was the most important command in the law of Moses, Jesus replied, "Love the Lord your God with all your heart, soul, and mind. This is the first and greatest commandment. The second most important is similar: 'Love your neighbor as much as you love yourself'" Matthew 22:37-39 (LB). Bottom line, God wants us to love Him and others. The home is the best place to teach children the meaning of love.

Of course, instruction must occur around unavoidable issues such as death, loss of friends or property due to typical life changes or a sudden calamity, routine successes and failures, peer pressure, bullying, substance abuse, respect for people in authority or others who are different, sexuality, stranger danger, and the like. Teachable moments are always presenting themselves related to these matters, and parents should do their level best to broach these important topics in timely, age-appropriate ways. The rigors of 21st-century parenting require intentionality when instructing children pertaining to things related to the Lord and previously cited subjects.

So, since it's imperative that you teach your children about a variety of things, how can you be most effective in this crucial role? Well, let me say this: it's certainly not by lecturing children 24/7. They'll tune you out. When we adults ramble on and on in lecture mode, what we say goes in one ear and out the other. There's a time and place for a good lecture; if not, we would not have Jesus' magnificent example, the Sermon on the Mount (the Beatitudes) recorded in Matthew 5:1-12 and Luke 6:20-23. But what parents and other concerned adults would do well to emulate are some of Jesus' other teaching methods. The following salient points are from an Internet article written by Brandon Hilgemann dated 7/05/18, entitled, *9 Teaching Methods of Jesus.*[6]

1. Jesus spoke by His authority (Matthew 5:22,28,32,39,44). He could do this because He is the Word (John 1). All authority on heaven and earth has been given to Him (Matthew 28:18).
2. Jesus told stories. He told countless parables. Jesus pulled stories from everyday life. The stories made Jesus' teaching more memorable, and they also connected in a more pro-found way. Some examples include the Prodigal Son, the

Good Samaritan, the Woman at the Well, and the Rich Young Ruler.

3. Jesus shocked people. He used hyperbole. He made outrageous, shocking statements to get people's attention. These statements were not to be taken literally but to get a point across. Here are a few examples: "Rip out your eyes or amputate your hands for causing us to sin" (Matthew 5:29,30). Jesus didn't mean people literally had logs in their eyes (Matthew 7:3-5).

4. Jesus crafted memorable sayings. He spoke poetically. He used catchy sayings and plays on words. Consider these examples: Judge not, and you will not be judged... (Luke 6:37-38a), Do to others as you would have them do to you (the Golden Rule) (Luke 6:31).

5. Jesus asked questions. Instead of just telling everyone the answer, Jesus led His listeners to conclusions by asking a lot of questions. Excellent examples of this method are demonstrated in Matthew 16:26, 22:20. "For what profit is it to a man if he gains the whole world, and loses his own soul?" "Whose image and inscription are this?"

6. Jesus used visual illustrations. He often used object lessons to communicate a point, a concrete truth, to His listeners. Jesus washed the feet of His disciples to teach servant leadership (John 13:3-17). He brought a little child forward to discuss childlike faith (Matthew 18:1-4). He described unselfish giving by calling attention to a widow as she dropped two small coins into the temple offering (Mark 12:41-44).

7. Jesus used repetition. Jesus helped His followers understand and remember His teachings by the use of frequent repetition. He taught the same major themes again and again, for example, death and resurrection (Mark 8:31, 9:31, 10:33-34)

8. Jesus created experiences. It wasn't enough for people to just listen to His teachings; Jesus gave instructions and called

> them to do what He said. He sent His followers out and then
> had them report back when they were done (Luke 10:1-11,17)
> 9. Jesus practiced what He preached. Jesus did not just teach
> about prayer. He often withdrew to a solitary place to pray
> (Luke 5:16). Jesus didn't just teach about loving sinners; He
> had dinner with them (Matthew 9:10-12). Jesus lived what He
> said. He didn't just talk a good talk; He walked the walk, even
> up to and including death on a cross.

You may be asking, "Can I use any or all the previously mentioned methods of Jesus as I instruct my children?" Of course, you can. You have the power of the Holy Spirit, your eternal guide and helper, to assist you. God will enable you to teach your children in a way that pleases Him and is uniquely suited to your children. It is by God's design that children are given to parents and placed under their authority. Use your authoritative position judiciously and lovingly, never heavy-handedly. Ephesians 6:1 states emphatically, "Children, obey your parents in the Lord, for this is right." As you stand on the unshakeable, eternal truth of God's Word, you're on a firm foundation that can never be eroded by trends and fads. Be sure to tell your children stories, all sorts of stories. The stories you tell or have your children listen to or read should include Bible stories, stories about people in their own family, stories about famous Christians, stories about people with impeccable character, stories about people who overcome great adversity, and even stories about people who use poor judgment. As stated earlier, stories are memorable, and they connect in profound ways. Stories can be shared orally by you or someone on a podcast or radio program, on TV via movies, or by reading together. Sometimes, a catchy children's song tells a great story. With a little planning, you can get your child to engage with the story before, during, and after through the use of questions that stimulate your child's thinking. Hyperbole can be extremely impactful, but the use of this method is best reserved for children who realize that you're not speaking literally. Hyperbole typically doesn't work for a seven-year-old. Age-appropriateness is vitally important when using the shock factor that Jesus utilized so deftly.

So, what about crafting memorable sayings? You may not have to scratch your head on this one because there are so many adages that have been passed down from generation to generation, like "practice makes perfect," or "if at first you don't succeed, try, try again," or "haste makes waste." Perhaps your family is like mine, where certain sayings are ascribed to a particular person like my dad who always used to say, "He who will not listen must feel," and "Habit is stronger than reasoning," or my grandma, "A place for everything and everything in its place," or my cousin, "Anything beats a blank," or the little poem my mother recited on many an occasion to reinforce her thinking, "If a task has once begun, never leave it till it's done. Be the labor great or small, do it well or not at all." I happen to love the expression, "Teamwork makes the dream work," and when using a phrase like that coupled with repetition, one of the other methods used by Jesus, you can definitely get the message across. Some phrases or Scripture passages are so meaningful that posting them around the house on plaques or something that stays in view is very useful. Since repetition is so valuable in making a point stick, try mixing things up with the use of poetry, music, games, and other fun activities. Another method that you should definitely use far more frequently than lecturing all the time is asking age-appropriate questions like, "Do you think God likes it when you...?" or "What would you do if one of your classmates needed a friend?" or "Have you ever felt that way?" Wait for your child's answer, and even if you're stunned or disappointed by their response, at least you know what they're thinking, and that's a great jumping-off point for further discussion.

Try to capitalize on visual illustrations as much as possible to emphasize your point. Here's an example from my daughters' childhood, one that they still talk about even though they're now in their fifties. While they were teenagers, I kept trying to drive the point across that their appearance was important and that, sad to say, many people do judge us by our appearance. So, one day, they came back home to find the smell of brownies filling the house. I showed them some brownies covered with powdered sugar presented on a decorative plate atop a beautiful doily and, by contrast, a few brownies set on top of a greasy, grimy garbage can lid that didn't even have a doily. I asked them, "Now, which presentation is the one that gives the best impression?" As I think back on this example, I probably shocked them with this visual illustration, so much so that the lesson was memorable enough that they remember it to the present day. As you go through your day-to-day activities, there will be countless teachable moments that you can seize to teach or reemphasize something that's already been taught to your children.

Finally, take time to create memorable teaching experiences for your children. Family service projects are great ways to do this. You can engage in a variety of helpful activities for an elderly neighbor, like providing meals, taking out trash cans, raking leaves, shoveling snow, bringing in groceries, and running errands. Your family can volunteer at a local food pantry, work to raise money, or collect books and/or clothing for people in need. I actually know a single mom who takes time once a month to cook food with her elementary-age children, helping her prepare the meals. Then, they serve the food together to some of the homeless people in her city. Think of all the valuable lessons her children learn through this recurring activity. The possibilities are endless. Continue to seek the Lord in prayer about what you can do to instruct your children about the things they need to know to grow in grace and the knowledge and truth of our Lord and Savior, Jesus Christ. Ask the Lord's guidance for the best ways to instruct your children about the countless things they need to know to successfully navigate various situations in life.

By way of summary, seriously consider the Lord's mandate to diligently teach your children. Prayerfully instruct them with intentionality day in and day out so your children are primarily learning from you the important aspects of kingdom living and what it takes to live successfully in a fallen, sin-cursed world. The time your children spend under your roof from birth to age eighteen, when many venture off to college, is a mere 6,574 days. You actually have less time than this because children spend time away with relatives and friends; they have overnight field trips and summer camp experiences, sleepovers at a friend's house, and other situations that result in them being away from you. When your children are young, it's easy to foolishly think you have all the time in the world to instruct them in the things of the Lord and other crucial matters of daily living. Take it from me, time spent with children seems to melt away faster than an ice cube in a hot cup of tea. Make the most of the time you have during your child's formative years. This is the prime time when children are most impressionable and moldable.

Day in and day out, many voices are vying for your child's attention, endeavoring to teach them something. On far too many occasions, those voices are not teaching good things. While watching *The View* on February 26, 2024, I heard Dr. Phil say, "You're not the only voice in your child's ear, so you need to be the best voice."[7] I hope that quote resonates with you as it did with me. Your work is to help mold your children into Christ's image. Make a concerted effort with your diligent teaching to have every day count for the cause of Christ. In Proverbs 4:13 (NIV), it says, "Hold on to instruction, do not let it go; guard it well, for it is your life." God will never cease to instruct us if we remain teachable. One of our principal goals as parents or other adults concerned about the welfare of children should be lifelong learning. As we remain open to learning, we are in the best position to successfully instruct our children in the areas of life that matter most.

ENCOURAGEMENT

Writer and statesman Johann Wolfgang von Goethe wisely said, "Instruction does much, but encouragement does more."[8] When children feel defeated and barely have hope that they will accomplish their goals or even make minimal progress toward something they want or need to do, discouragement or, worse yet, despair sets in. That's when encouragement is sorely needed. According to Doug Fields, an author of numerous books on youth ministry, "Words of encouragement build confidence, discouraging words destroy hope." What parent purposefully sets out to dash her child's hopes and dreams? Yet that's what can happen over time. Can we live without oxygen? Of course not! Encouragement is like oxygen. Encouragement urges a child on, gives him hope, increases her confidence, and provides the emotional support that keeps the child pressing on toward their goals. Children should know that the adults in their lives, especially their parents, are in their corner whether they succeed or fail. When we encourage children, we accentuate the positive instead of harping on the negative. Being negative all the time makes children feel you don't like them and, in some instances, that you don't really love them. Who in their right mind wants to be around people who don't like them? How can loving relationships thrive in the midst of a barrage of negativity? You may tell your children you love them, but by your words and deeds, do they think you like them? There are always opportunities to joyously encourage children by stressing or focusing on their strengths. When weaknesses seem to be creating havoc in day-to-day activities, even small improvements can be cause for celebration and great joy. Jesus says in John 15:11 (NIV), "I have told you this so that my joy may be in you and that your joy may be complete." Speak encouraging words to your children on a daily basis, and you'll see that it brings joy into their lives and yours.

Encouragement can take the form of affirmation (words of praise or inspiration, hugs and kisses, pats on the back, high fives, or thumbs up, etc.) and rewards (something given in recognition of a good deed). Both positive affirmations and rewards are motivators when used correctly. Both forms of encouragement bring joy into the lives of recipients.

Affirmation extends recognition to the child for demonstrating desired attitudes and actions. For example, if a child usually doesn't share his toys, even when urged to do so, then it's important to encourage the right response whenever it occurs. The following instances are examples of behaviors that could result in encouragement for a child when he:

- **Exceeds standards** - Your son Jeffrey cleans up his room and helps his sister clean her room as well. You might say something as simple as, "Jeffrey, I noticed you not only cleaned up your room, but you helped Ashley with her room as well. Good job!"
- **Consistently meets standards** - Jeffrey completes all chores as directed on a regular basis. Your remark could be, "Jeffrey, I want you to know I appreciate how I don't have to chase after you to do your chores. You're on it, son."
- **Meets standards not usually met** - Jeffrey passes the first math test after failing previous quizzes and tests. Perhaps you can say something like, "Jeffrey, your hard work with the tutor and all the extra time studying are paying off. If you can keep this up, I think you're going to pass math this marking period."
- **Makes an improvement in meeting standards** - Jeffrey takes a shower without being told to do so, even though he still needs to be reminded to wash out the tub. Some

encouraging words might be, "Jeffrey, way to go jumping right in the shower after basketball practice. Great-smelling cologne. Try to remember to wash out the tub right away so it's clean for the next person."

You can also follow up your specific words of encouragement with non-verbal praise such as a smile, a pat on the back, or a high five. One other quick note: always offer your words of encouragement with sincerity and enthusiasm.

Before you read further, pause and take a moment to think about something one of your children did recently that falls into one of the four previously cited categories. Did you take time to offer words of encouragement when you first observed the behavior? If so, great! If not, make a mental note of what you can say to your child and deliver that positive message as soon as you can. Try to get your child's undivided attention when offering your words or gestures of encouragement to ensure that what you're saying or doing isn't lost in the shuffle of daily distractions. You might consider writing down your words of encouragement so your child can reread the sentiment you expressed at some other point in the future. When you offer words of affirmation, you let children know that their efforts are noticed and appreciated, and that keeps them moving along to becoming the children God wants them to be.

A reward or bonus incentive can take the form of:
- Special privileges (staying up a little later)
- Gifts (receiving something that brings joy or excitement)
- Money (receiving a little extra money to spend on something the child wants)
- Activities (going to a special event)

When a child does something over and above what is asked of him or recognizes a need and responds without being told, that is appropriate behavior to reward. A child who works hard to please those in authority for the sake of doing what's right, rather than expecting to gain something in exchange for her efforts, is a candidate for a reward.

Encouragement helps children garner the strength to continue with the daily grind of learning new things, taking on more and more responsibilities, and combating obstacles. Daily words of encouragement give children the boost they need to persevere when the going gets tough, which it will on many occasions. Perseverance is crucial to success. Encouragement strengthens a child's resolve to keep at it until what she needs or wants to do is accomplished. A favorite quote of a dear friend of mine is, "Encouragement sweetens labor." Lavish encouragement in the right settings and in the right way, and see the joyous, positive results that come from that approach. Encouragement is a relatively easy way to help modify or shape your children's behavior.

"Today is a good day for planting: bulbs for daffodils in the spring. A twig for a someday tree; loving thoughts and words of praise in the heart of a child." ~ Author Unknown. Make it your mission to pursue opportunities on a daily basis to be an encouragement to your children. Your loving words of praise and appropriate rewards will help your children bloom where they're planted, and what a blessing that will be for your family and other people your children meet.

CORRECTION

What car owner, knowing the importance of heeding panel lights, ignores the check engine light for a prolonged period of time? When that happens, the ensuing problem is huge. The engine seizes, resulting in the costly repair or replacement of the engine. When the warning light appears initially, that's the time to immediately look into the problem and take the necessary corrective steps to remedy the situation. Hang in there with me as I draw a parallel to what's happening in many families today. Because children's inappropriate or alarming behavior is being ignored or dismissed, huge unintended consequences are surfacing in the home, at church, at school, at sports venues, and at other extracurricular locations. Bullying at school and in cyberspace, children operating with a sense of entitlement, and pervasive cheating and conniving to attain accomplishments are just a few of the problems on full display these days. Perhaps parents are uninformed about the potential long-term effects of misbehavior that go unchecked, or maybe they think there's no need to take corrective measures immediately. Perhaps they're afraid they'll alienate their children, or maybe they're just too preoccupied with other professional or personal matters to address challenging situations in a timely fashion. Could it be that some parents naively think their children will outgrow the inappropriate behavior that relatives, teachers, and youth leaders are constantly bringing to their attention? The reasons for parental inaction make no difference. The result is the same; like an ignored check engine light, there will always be bigger problems to deal with in the long run. Failing to take intentional corrective measures at the outset will be extremely problematic as issues persist.

Correction is the act or process of setting right, the counteracting of harmful effects. Correction is the God-given responsibility of parents and other adults in authority to help children eliminate errors and faults, so they align with God's standards. Correction enables children to grow up to be the productive, successful adults God intends for them to be. It's the Lord who definitively says in Jeremiah 29:11, "'For I know the plans I have for you,' declares the Lord, 'plans to prosper you and not to harm you, plans to give you hope and a future.'" Since we read in Psalm 127:3 (NLT) that "Children are a gift from the Lord, they are a reward from him," we can rest assured that God's plans for children are good. He has the highest intentions and purest motives when it comes to children. His thoughts are superior to ours when it relates to what children can ultimately become. Correction supports God's highest aims for your children's future.

As far as the Christian faith is concerned, the Bible is clear about the purpose of correction. We see in Hebrews 12:5-11 (LB) the following: "And have you quite forgotten the encouraging words that God spoke to you, his child? He said, 'My son, don't be angry when the Lord punishes you. Don't be discouraged when he has to show you where you are wrong. For when he punishes you, it proves that he loves you. When he whips you, it proves you are really his child.' Let God train you, for he is doing what any loving father does for his children. Whoever heard of a son who was never corrected? If God doesn't punish you when you need it, as other fathers punish their sons, then it means that you aren't really God's son at all-that you don't belong in his family. Since we respect our fathers here on earth, though they punish us, should we not all the more cheerfully submit to God's training so that we can begin to really live? Our earthly fathers trained us for a few brief years, doing the best for us that they knew how, but God's correction is always right and best for our good, that we may share his holiness. Being punished isn't enjoyable when it is happening-it hurts! But afterwards we can see the result, a quiet growth in grace and character."

In the previously cited text, God warns us not to despise God's correction. We are not to make light of it or lose heart when the Lord enacts corrective measures in our lives. Warnings or advice against something should be taken seriously, just like the check engine light should be taken seriously. Warnings are critically important for children, but perpetual warnings are no substitute for correction. The bottom line, God corrects His children because He loves us and wants us to be holy like Him. The Lord wants His children to be the partakers of the abundant blessings of righteousness. Job 5:17-18 (NIV) states, "Blessed is the one whom God corrects; so, do not despise the chastening of the Almighty. For he wounds, but he also binds up; he injures, but His hands also heal." Just as the Lord corrects us for our own good, parents and other concerned adults must be willing to correct children for their own good because we desire the best for them as well. It's because we love our children and want to see them follow in the ways of the Lord that we must correct them.

How can correction best be accomplished in the home? Is spanking an acceptable form of correction for children in the 21st century? The debate about spanking and other corrective measures has raged on for decades. Research studies have been conducted, and many experts in the field of child psychology have written opinion papers about the harmful effects of spanking. For example, the American Psychological Association featured an article entitled, "The Case Against Spanking" by Brendan L. Smith in the April 2012, Vol. 43, No. 4 journal, which states that physical discipline has been slowly declining as some studies reveal lasting harms for children.[9] Many studies have shown that physical punishment, which includes spanking, can lead to physical injury, anti-social behavior, mental health problems, etc. Still, surveys show that nearly two-thirds of Americans approve of spanking children. Dr. Alan E. Kazdin, formerly a Yale University psychology professor and director of the Yale Parenting Center and Child Conduct Center, stated emphatically in Smith's article that spanking doesn't work. He is quoted as saying, "You cannot punish out these behaviors that you do not want." Dr. Kazdin believes spanking is a horrible and ineffective technique that does not work. Dr. Kazdin's research has focused primarily on the treatment of aggressive and antisocial behavior. He is the recipient of countless awards, including the American Psychological Association Lifetime Award for his contributions to the field of psychology. As the author of over 40 books and a facilitator of his online Parent Management Training courses, Dr. Kazdin is deemed a subject matter expert and a great resource for struggling parents.

Let me be perfectly clear: I concur that certain forms of physical punishment will absolutely result in very harmful effects on children.

I have seen that over and over again during my years as a career educator. However, even experts in the field admit that research studies have some shortcomings. Research on parental discipline will largely be correlational in nature since children cannot be randomly assigned to parents for the purpose of an experiment. Controversies about the topic of spanking will never cease, I'm sure. But there's no getting around this fact: parents will have to make their own determinations about what forms of correction will be utilized in their homes because correction will be necessary at some point and should not be avoided. Correcting misbehavior should not be administered off the cuff, with a "knee-jerk" reaction. Knee-jerk doesn't work! Parents should endeavor to correct their children with intentionality, constantly considering how a loving God would want them to correct the children He's entrusted to their care.

To facilitate your consideration regarding corrective measures, a distinction will be made between Biblical chastisement and cultural spanking:

Biblical chastisement, one form of correction, is not something you do to the child but something you do for the child. Proverbs 22:15 says, "Foolishness is bound up in the heart of the child, the rod of correction will drive it far from him." Proverbs 23:13 and 14 (NIV) state, "Do not withhold discipline from a child; if you punish them with the rod, they will not die. Punish them with the rod and save them from death." And finally, Proverbs 13:24 (NIV) tells us, "Whoever spares the rod hates their children, but the one who loves their children is careful to discipline them."

Cultural spanking, on the other hand, is something you do to the child. It is often humiliating, abusive, and destructive. Invariably, this is the type of spanking experts are evaluating in their research studies and writing opinions about.

As seen in the previously cited verses in Proverbs, the Bible directs parents to chastise their children, specifically by using a "rod of correction." According to Dictionary.com, the definition of chastise is "to discipline, especially by corporal punishment."[10] As already mentioned, child psychologists frown on corporal punishment and vehemently oppose its use. Because so many parents - and you may number among them - have had devastating childhood experiences related to spanking at the hands of their parents or other adults, they often shy away from the use of any form of corporal punishment with their children. Instead, they rely on other, in some instances, less effective methods when correcting their children.

It's normal to wrestle with the topic of spanking, something that parents and children have dealt with for generations. Because of my age and the prominent role spanking played in child-rearing in the 1950s and 1960s, I wondered what younger parents were thinking about the subject these days. During my growing-up years, not only did your parents spank you, but aunties and uncles and neighbors and friends had carte blanche to "whip your tail," too, if you were caught doing the wrong thing. I was so curious about the thinking among today's parents that I gathered a focus group together, and I conducted a number of one-on-one phone interviews to talk about spanking. All of the participants were Gen Xers (those born between 1966 and 1980) or Millennials (those born in the 1980s or 1990s). The contributors are highly functioning, professionally successful adults, the overwhelming majority of whom have advanced degrees. I posed the following questions:

- What were your childhood experiences related to spanking?
- How did your experiences influence the way you spank or refrain from spanking your children?
- What other resources related to spanking informed your decision-making on the topic?
- What discussions about spanking have you had with your children?

- How effective was spanking in curbing your misbehavior/your children's misbehavior?
- What, if any, opinions about spanking have your children expressed to you?

Here's what they told me:

All contributors to the conversation were spanked. As one person put it, "Good Lord, I was spanked." The millennials were spanked to a far lesser degree. However, both generations, in particular the millennials, felt they were the beneficiaries of changes in child-rearing philosophies that occurred over time, as a lot more talking transpired to try to achieve better outcomes. Childhood curiosity was encouraged and not punished. The Gen Xers were spanked in keeping with cultural, regional, and familial traditions. Two participants brought up interesting insights about their parents and relatives who grew up in the South and didn't hesitate to "whip their tails." One person said, "This type of behavior was what they knew to do." The other person commented that perhaps it was a throwback to slavery days when children were "whipped" to prevent a far more horrific whipping from the master, or worse yet, being sold off the plantation away from their family. The Gen Xers were quick to point out that there was minimal talking before the actual spanking occurred because, in many instances, the spanking was administered out of sheer frustration. Spankings motivated by frustration were often done in public, adding the additional element of humiliation to the experience. Spankings were accomplished with the switch, one selected by the person doing the spanking or the one who was going to receive the spanking, wooden spoons, belts with buckles removed, and other assorted spanking tools. Many parents kept whatever they used for spanking in very convenient places like behind the car visor, on the back of the door, in purses, and so forth. Children were spanked to be kept in line, and in cases when the child was wrongfully spanked, the parent did not apologize. Blended families brought dual spankings for the same infraction, and seldom were the spankings carried out in the same way. So, the result was that many of the contributors spent time during their childhood in fear. They didn't want to anger, frustrate, or disappoint their parents, or do anything that would elicit a spanking. Even with all that, the participants were quick to say that because they received an abundance of demonstrated love and support, that was the counterbalance to the spankings.

So, how did the childhood experiences of the 15 interviewees affect how they spank or refrain from spanking? Only one participant did not spank at all. She was vehemently opposed to spanking.

There were many variations on the spanking theme, from a pop on the hand, a swat on the leg, to a serious spanking. Virtually all the female participants spoke about the "snatch," a technique used when children were in danger or out in public acting like fools. The snatch or "number one serious look" worked well when children were consistently disciplined at home. These parents talked about the importance of communicating clear expectations and quickly following up on infractions with some level of accountability. Giving time-outs, removing privileges, and seizing on teachable moments were among the other techniques used. Overall, I learned from the interviewees, especially the millennials, that they do a lot more talking to help children understand why their behavior is unacceptable.

But one thing everyone agreed on was that children growing up today are far less respectful of adults, as exhibited in their tone of voice when speaking to parents and those in authority, and in their outright disobedient actions. The respondents thought that it was because the children did not have a healthy fear of their parents.

When the question was posed about what other resources informed people's decision-making related to spanking, few contributors took formal courses or attended workshops covering the topic. There were, however, a few participants whose professions required training in child development and related topics, and they stated that the points of view presented in their coursework were a benefit to them.

One contributor attended the *Blueprint* workshop with his wife on two different occasions and stated that the tools presented in the workshop were very impactful. Some people read books or watched videos about spanking, but not to any great degree. It seemed like the advice of family members and friends had the greatest influence on the contributors after their own personal experiences.

I found it very interesting that discussions with children concerning spanking were few and far between. It seemed like the greatest concern was related to not lecturing the children when parents decided to spank them. These parents held to their position that a spanking was in order and did not hesitate to briefly explain to their children why that was the case.

As far as children's reactions to spankings, some contributors told me that their children said the spankings didn't hurt or mentioned they preferred to be spanked by one parent rather than the other parent. The participants didn't elaborate on the reason why their children felt that way. Some children spoke up when they thought they were undeserving of a spanking, and certain children even thanked their parents for correcting them. In most instances, the children hadn't expressed specific opinions about being spanked.

The answers to the question about how effective spanking was at curbing misbehavior seemed to span the gamut from it wasn't effective at all, to it was a deterrent because there was dread for the 'physical doom' that was coming. Respondents stated that they firmly believe fear factors impact how the child perceives love from their parents. One contributor was clear to say the one spanking she administered to a nephew seemed to break his spirit. Some participants believed measured spankings were effective because their children were open to their correction and were quick to confide in them. There seemed to be universal agreement that even with the potential shortcomings of spanking children, this form of correction still resulted in the following benefits:

- It fostered respect.
- It reinforced parameters and boundaries.
- It instilled the importance of following orders.

The previously cited information is purely anecdotal in nature and hopefully provides some food for thought as you wrestle with the topic of spanking. What jumped out at me after interacting with the Gen Xers and Millennials that I was privileged to speak with is this: spanking, in particular Biblical chastisement, has been and still is largely misunderstood and misapplied. Much of what was being done or not done in the area of spanking was largely due to familial, cultural, or societal traditions, peer opinions, and personal experiences, many of which were quite negative. Man's ways and God's ways are usually diametrically opposed, and that certainly is the case with regard to spanking.

What follows in this section is information from a Biblical perspective about when, why, and how it's advantageous to chastise children. You will also see specific suggestions about what to do when you chastise your children, so your methods do not displease God or harm your children physically or psychologically in the process.

As you view Biblical chastisement and cultural spanking side by side, you'll notice distinct differences. As it relates to spanking, consider your own childhood experiences as well as your children's experiences with you if you use spanking as a corrective measure.

Ask yourself, am I correcting my children Biblically or culturally?

Biblical Chastisement	Cultural Chastisement[11]
Initiated by child's rebellion	Initiated by parent frustration
Instituted out of love	Instituted out of anger as a last resort
Application of controlled efforts	Application of uncontrolled efforts
Clears child's guilty conscience	Frustrates, exasperates the child
Is used to change inward attitudes	Is used to control outward behavior
Molds life-long character	Has limited positive effect
Leads to love and respect	Often leads to trauma, fear, abuse
Is nearly completed by age 5	Is performed throughout a child's life
Is rarely used	Is frequently used by Christians and non-Christians

I asked you to consider your own childhood experiences and your children's experiences as you looked at Biblical chastisement and cultural spanking side by side, and I hope you did that at various points while viewing the contrasting approaches. Did you have a reason to pause and truly reflect on your current approach to spanking? As I recall my own strict upbringing, how could I ever forget that I definitely had my share of spankings, and with a barber strap, no less? I think my parents' corrective methods were more of a hodge-podge approach than anything else. For the most part, I was an obedient little girl growing up, as I was not looking forward to an encounter with the barber strap. My son and daughter had different experiences with me as I became more familiar with Biblical chastisement. I wasn't a Christian for the first nine years of my daughter's life, and even after becoming a Christian, I wasn't exposed to God's blueprint for raising children at the outset of my Christian journey. My dear daughter got many a spanking out of frustration. I'm ashamed to recount two different incidents. In one instance, I hit her at every traffic light after I had to leave my job in NY and travel home to NJ to pick her up from after-school detention that she failed to tell me she had to serve. And then there's the time I almost tore the door off the hinges when I was barreling into her room to really give it to her for Lord knows what. My son, on the other hand, was wisely disciplined using Biblical chastisement. We both still chuckle at a time when he was about six and, with pleading eyes, said, "Mommy, I prefer mercy and not justice." I had to turn my face to the wall when I told him I'd prayerfully consider his request. I did, and I gave him two fewer "whacks" than I'd originally intended. You'll see how his request factored into my decision-making after you read the next part of this section, which provides a step-by-step approach to Biblical Chastisement.

How To Approach Biblical Chastisement

1. Chastise **privately**. Public spankings, even in your own home in front of other people, are humiliating and ill-advised.

2. **Pray**. Prayer has a calming effect on you and gives God an opportunity to adjust your thinking and correct any wrong attitudes you may have.

3. Establish the child's guilt. A very young child should be told what he did wrong. An older child should be required to state what she did wrong.

4. Use the Bible to show the child the error of her ways. Quote a verse of Scripture that applies to the situation. It may also be helpful to cite a verse from Proverbs that establishes the need for spanking. Tell the child in your own way that you love her too much to let the wrongdoing continue.

(Steps 3 and 4 should be deliberate but not long and drawn out. Keep the tone **calm and conversational** and use direct eye contact throughout this phase).

5. Spank the child with a "rod of correction" that has flex to it. The advantage of using an instrument with flex is that it will sting without inflicting serious injury. It seems that the "old school" approach of having a child choose his own "switch" from among the backyard tree branches contained a lot of wisdom. That certainly allowed for some time and distance before the spanking occurred. **AVOID USING YOUR HAND.** A child should associate parents' hands with **love, provision, and protection**, not pain. **NEVER** slap a child's face, pull his hair, beat, kick, shake, or punch him violently.

6. (The number of "swats" or "whacks" should relate to the child's age and the seriousness of the offense. Usually, you can get the point across with 1-5 swats).

7. When the spanking is complete, give the child a few moments to calm himself. Re-establish fellowship with a hug. Assure the child of your forgiveness and love. If the child asks for forgiveness, grant it, and do not bring up the matter again.

8. Pray with your child and end with brief words of encouragement. Try to get things back to normal quickly. **Consider the matter closed.**

So, what type of behavior qualifies for chastisement? **Rebellion!** Rebellion is a heart issue that includes disobedience of any kind, disrespect, and bad attitudes. Rebellion can be active or passive. Active rebellion consists of disobedience, talking back, or refusing to accept correction, while passive rebellion is a lot more subtle and includes pouting, whining, or sulking. Parents should never use Biblical chastisement as presented above for childish behavior like soiling clothes, misplacing something, or accidentally breaking an object. Those types of issues may warrant some sort of punishment depending on the scenario and the child's age.

Some people use chastisement and punishment interchangeably. These are not interchangeable terms. There is one form of Biblical chastisement and many forms of punishment.

Punishment is the penalty imposed for unacceptable behavior like lying, stealing, disregarding other people's property, greed, laziness, bullying, cursing, etc. Some forms of punishment include privilege removal, repayment with money and/or labor, sending a child to his room for a time-out, etc. Punishment should be a fitting retribution for the offense. For example, if an older child is careless with a sibling's toy and breaks it, then she should have to replace that toy, even if it means doing work to earn some extra allowance to do so. If a child carelessly misplaces something or doesn't put it back in its proper place, the child should be restricted from using that object for a period of time and then reminded to put the object back in its proper place where it belongs before the next permitted use.

Avoid dual penalties such as spanking plus taking away privileges unrelated to an offense, as these actions are often counter-productive. For example, if a child fails to put the garbage curbside on the days of his specified week, he could be required to do that chore for an entire month instead of alternating the chore with a sibling. Spanking the child, taking away his phone, or employing some other action, like doing other unrelated chores, will probably not register with the child and likely breed some resentment.

Another form of punishment that seems to be growing in prevalence these days is "shaming." Far too many parents weaponize their words, continually pummeling their children with a barrage of insults and negative commentary. Do these parents think calling their children "losers," "dummies," "useless," and far worse is going to correct whatever is irritating the parent at that moment? Hardly! This type of irresponsible and exasperating shaming will only compound the problem.

Before you conclude reading this section, please engage in a SELAH moment. I am suggesting you pause to answer two questions:

1. What is the most important "takeaway" that I picked up from what I just read?
2. What am I going to do differently as a result of that "takeaway?"

Perhaps one of your "takeaways" is that you must never again spank your child out of anger or frustration. Maybe your heart is convicted that you won't ever spank your child anywhere but in a private setting. Or, in light of what you read, you now think spanking has a place in the parenting process because God mentions spanking in the Bible. Of course, it is great to come to some important conclusions, and to have your own eureka moment, but it is not enough to leave the next steps to simply be changing your thinking about something. You must do something different. Depending on the age of your child, you may need to humble yourself and ask their forgiveness for your anger or frustration-driven spankings of the past. There may be a need to have a serious discussion with your children about God's perspective as it relates to spanking. When all is said and done, you'll need the Spirit of the Living God to fall afresh on you in this area, so future corrective measures are truly guided by the Lord.

I can assure you God will speak to your heart if you take the time to sit still before Him. If you inquire of God earnestly about what you should be doing differently with regard to this particular aspect of your parenting, God will make the way forward very clear to you. This is not about what your parents, peers, experts, or other miscellaneous folks are saying or doing regarding spanking. This is about your commitment to doing things God's way, which is very hard at times because God's way is usually counterintuitive and counter-cultural.

Correction is a vital part of everyone's life journey, and it certainly is a critical component of the child-rearing process. When parents and responsible adults use chastisement and punishment appropriately, consistently, and out of a heart of love, children learn to line up to God's standards. Adults are responsible for heightening a child's understanding of the need for correction. Adults should be disciplined and intentional in their approach when it comes to doling out corrective measures. They can ill afford to be haphazard when there's so much at stake. Wisdom from God's word is a great reminder as we read in Proverbs 10:17 (NIV), "Whoever heeds discipline shows the way of life, but whoever ignores correction leads others astray." Parents who are willing to embrace God's correction in their own lives will be better suited to correct their children properly. Proverbs 3:11 and 12 should be repeated often so children see that they must not despise the Lord's discipline nor resent His reprimand because the Lord disciplines those He loves. Since godly parents love their children and want them to gain knowledge, wisdom, and understanding, they discipline them using God-ordained correction, truly believing the appropriate use of a "rod of correction" is a type of "wisdom worker." God would never ordain an abusive measure to discipline His children. Remember that Biblical chastisement never borders on being abusive, humiliating, or psychologically damaging. This type of correction stems from a heart of love, God's love, for what is deemed best for children from God's perspective. You must strive to gain godly wisdom when it comes to correcting your children. Think often about Proverbs 3:15, which tells us that wisdom is more precious than rubies and nothing one can desire can compare with her. Do you really believe that? If so, do you act on your belief?

I bet you consider your life and the lives of the precious children you interact with more valuable than whatever car you drive. Typically, adults are more cognizant of driving safely when children are riding with them; they want to avoid a car wreck at all costs. But consider this: if you were dangerously speeding down the road with children in your car, darting in and out of traffic, would it surprise you if flashing lights came out of nowhere, signaling you to pull over? Hopefully, you'd feel the traffic stop was warranted because not only were you endangering your life, the lives of the children in your vehicle, but other people's lives as well. The subsequent ticket and points on your license are designed to be a deterrent for that type of imprudent behavior when you get behind the wheel in the future. It's a corrective measure that should be embraced and not despised. If, as adults, we need measures to help us gain prudence in the ways we conduct ourselves, how much more do growing and evolving children need the adults in their lives to exercise their God-given authority to correct them? Correction will help children gain godly wisdom and align with the standards God has for their lives. When that happens, children are blessed, and so is everyone who comes in contact with them.

COUNSELING

It's the Lord who is the righteous role model, the superior standard bearer, the one we should emulate on a day-to-day basis. But too often, we fall far short of the glory of God. There are times we try so hard to adhere to what God wants us to do, but to no avail. The hard truth is this: **all** have sinned and come short of the glory of God (Romans 3:23). Have you ever been in that dark place where your flesh failings loomed large over your life like an enormous, expansive shadow? I know I've been there, weeping and wailing and lamenting all the mistakes I made, especially as it related to how I was parenting at the time. I knew in the very core of my soul that a course correction was in order, yet I was at my wit's end as to what particular course to embark on. But I am so grateful that God's long and strong arm has the power to reach us in the darkest, gloomiest places of our lives to guide and direct us to His transcendent light. God's light can and will illumine our pathway and show us the way forward. Since God is no respecter of persons, I know what He's done for me and countless others, He'll do for you.

God is the Wonderful Counselor. A counselor is an advisor, someone who makes recommendations that guide us to appropriate courses of action. As it says in Psalm 73:24 (NLT), "You guide me with your counsel, leading me to a glorious destiny." Our Wonderful Counselor uses a variety of methods to guide us. I truly believe that some of the most under-utilized resources that His people fail to tap into are counsel from the Word of God and advice from mature Christians who uphold God's ways. In certain circumstances, guidance based on the expertise that a Biblical counselor brings to the table is warranted. There are many times in our lives when undergoing formal counseling would be extremely advantageous. Instead, we let the stigma associated with counseling or the money and/or time we think we don't have to get in the way of seeking the help we desperately need. Our wrong thinking about advice from certain sources, especially professional Christian counselors, becomes a true impediment to the progress that God wants us to make in our lives. It's God who says in Proverbs 19:20, "Listen to counsel and receive instruction, that you may be wise in your latter days." Another verse to contemplate is Proverbs 1:5, which states, "A wise man will hear and increase learning, and a man of understanding will attain wise counsel." That advice from God's Word should suffice to motivate us to seek sound counsel. Instead, we oftentimes stumble along in life, making one poor choice after another. And where does that get us? Rather than soaring to the heavenly heights where we can obtain the outstanding outcomes God intends for us, we're slowly but surely being sucked deeper and deeper into the quicksand that brings death to relationships, dreams, and opportunities. I recognized when I was drowning in the deep waters of my troubled family situation that I had to seek wise counsel. The Lord provided older, wiser women to help me in my predicament. I also sought and benefited from sessions with a Biblical counselor.

Biblical counseling gives guidance or advice about a particular situation from God's perspective. Who among us never needs guidance or good advice? The Bible speaks about the wisdom of obtaining advice in Proverbs 11:14, "Where no counsel is, the people fall: but in a multitude of counselors there is safety." At times, people will clearly see the necessity of seeking wise counsel. This is especially true when they're faced with complicated legal, financial, medical, or professional matters. But what about seeking wise counsel for one of the most important and challenging areas of life, training children in the way they should go? Proverbs 12:15 provides a warning and sound advice for us all as it relates to matters of daily living. It states, "The way of a fool is right in his own eyes, but he who heeds counsel is wise." It's a fool who thinks he can't benefit from the advice of others. Parents, especially first-time parents, should be open to the advice of knowledgeable people. Sad to say, one's family members, friends, prominent internet influencers, or secular subject matter experts may not be the best source of wise counsel when it comes to raising children. The caliber of the advice given is crucial to obtaining righteous recommendations for ways to avert disaster while navigating certain situations. Wise counsel helps us secure sacred solutions for the problems at hand. Shouldn't we want recommendations and solutions that have God's stamp of approval on them?

Obtaining godly counsel when you're in the thick of the most challenging aspects of the parenting process or engaged in any other complicated situation can accomplish a number of things:

- Offer valuable insights and righteous recommendations about ways to prevent problems from occurring or spiraling out of control.
- Give help by providing time-tested Biblical solutions to problems.
- Provide comfort and encouragement as you navigate problems in trying times.

Depending on the nature of the problem or matter under consideration, parents can receive godly counsel from another believer who possesses valuable insights about the issue, pastors or elders, Christian authors, godly subject matter experts, or professional Christian counselors. I offer this word of caution to Christian parents: avoid seeking guidance initially or exclusively from secular sources. Pray about the best counsel to seek. Humanistic approaches seldom point you to the time-tested warnings and solutions given in God's Word. In fact, in many instances, the suggestions offered are opposite to what God would have you do in that situation, and additional problems can result. Let me elaborate on my opinion by presenting some information gleaned from Dr. David L. Johnston's YouTube video and my personal experience studying Biblical Counseling and utilizing it over the years. In Dr. Johnston's video entitled "What is Christian Counseling?"[12], the following points are presented regarding Christian counseling:

1. Represents Christ
2. Represents the Holy Spirit
3. Represents the Word of God
4. Represents love

Even without watching the video for yourself to gain deeper insights, what you can see from the four points listed above is that Christian counseling represents God's highest order. With Jesus as the human embodiment of all that's good and perfect, the empowerment of the Holy Spirit who guides us to truth, the eternal truth presented in God's Word, with the ultimate aim of God's love being shed abroad in our hearts, how can a believer go wrong? Ponder for a moment the fact that God's unconditional and undeniable love is perfect. God's love is chasing us and wooing us day in and day out, even when we fail to see that's the case. As Dr. Johnston states, "His love is the unrelenting pursuit of the highest good of others until that highest pursuit becomes reality." With that in mind, God wants to make wrongs right in our lives, and His help toward that end is assured when we cry out to Him.

You might be wondering whether what you're grappling with merits a closer look at the potential benefits of formal counseling. You may be asking yourself, what are some of the typical issues people face that make them seek godly guidance? Here are some of the usual issues that mature Christians and professional Christian counselors help people deal with:

- Marital Infidelity
- Divorce
- Ongoing conflicts with family members
- Death of a loved one
- Sexual and physical abuse
- Addictions
- Childhood problems related to school, physical, and emotional trauma
- Teenage rebellion and sexual issues

Something on the list may have struck a chord with you. Good! That should help you see you're not alone in your struggles. Plenty of people are wrestling with a variety of challenges that have the capacity to pin them to the mat and bring about defeat. We need not fear or succumb to defeat as struggles come our way. We should expect struggles in this life. Jesus said in John 16:33 (LB), "I have told you all this so that you will have peace of heart and mind. Here on earth, you will have many trials and sorrows, but cheer up, for I have overcome the world." You can lean in and embrace your struggles and view them as the conduit to help you draw closer to our Victor over Satan's vast demonic domain. There is no problem you'll encounter in this world that you can't conquer with Christ's help.

So when you're embroiled in a struggle that is marked by confusion and conflict, or you're about to enter a particularly challenging period in the parenting process or another crucial area of your life, what can you do to be on the receiving end of the best advice or counsel possible? First, realize that since God is not the author of confusion, you need to turn to Him for the appropriate next steps. If your life is chaotic, God can make a way out of "no way" to bring you peace. You can have confident trust that He will help you uncover the best solutions to your problems. God provides solutions over time that will change your situation for the better. Jesus says in Luke 11:9 (NIV), "So I say to you, 'Ask and it will be given to you; seek, and you will find; knock and the door will be opened to you.'" I think the myriad of problems pummeling Christian parents today stem from the fact that many parents are looking for answers to their important questions and solutions for their problems in all the wrong places. I've heard it said by Christian parents on far too many occasions, "Oh well, I've tried lots of things, so I guess all I can do now is pray." I believe the very first and ongoing thing to do is pray. We're exhorted in God's Word to pray without ceasing. Pray for God's divine direction and perfect will in the matter at hand. God says **ask**, so do that! God will never fail or forsake you. Remember this: He wants to help you by proving Himself strong and mighty in the midst of your circumstances. Here is a precious promise from God's word in Isaiah 41:13 (NIV), which states, "For I am the Lord your God who takes hold of your right hand and says to you, 'Do not fear; I will help you.'" With God's help, you can conquer any and every challenge you currently face or will ever face in the future.

After you ask and continue to inquire about God's divine direction, actively **seek** out people, places, and things that can be of help to you. The Lord will guide you at every turn to find something or someone to assist you. Resources abound. Leaders in your church, godly family members and friends, books, YouTube videos, webinars and in-person seminars, podcasts, and Christian counselors are possible avenues for help. Because the choices are many, that's why you need divine discernment as to the best sources of help for your situation. If your current condition is messy and complicated, then there's a higher likelihood you'll need to seek help from a professional counselor or therapist. There's no shame in going that route. In fact, it will probably be one of the wisest decisions and best investments of time and money you'll ever make. Be sure to prayerfully consider and prudently select an experienced counselor. So, what factors are important as you try to zero in on a counselor to assist you? I believe the person you select should:

- Esteem God highly, believing He is omniscient (possessing all wisdom), omnipotent (all-powerful), omnipresent (present in all places), and mighty to save and deliver.
- Consider people as precious souls for whom Christ died, His unique creations worthy of love and respect.
- Be able to incorporate faith-based principles into the counseling process. The selected counselor must have the ability to help his or her clients understand how their beliefs impact various facets of their lives.
- Have strong knowledge of Scriptural passages that are relevant to daily living.

- Possess a solid, stable Christian testimony.
- Be prayerful and humble.
- Exercise compassion.
- Refrain from being judgmental or condemnatory.
- Engage counselees in realistic improvement strategies and/or recovery goals.
- Be committed to their own personal, professional, and spiritual growth.

What has been delineated may cause you to think it will be an almost impossible task to find the right counselor. Don't forget that God knows the person who possesses the perfect mix of characteristics to guide you along the way. As stated earlier, God will never fail or forsake you. He won't!

After you believe you've found the person you can trust to be your guiding influence, then **knock** on the door of their heart and expertise. You'll want their knowledge, wisdom, and understanding to be opened up for your benefit. They will pose all sorts of questions to get a handle on your situation. This is vitally necessary to enhance their understanding so they can make the best recommendations to help you obtain the positive results you seek. You'll need to be forthcoming and transparent with the information requested so your counselor can properly assess your current condition. Avoid blame-shifting and excuse-making as you answer the counselor's questions. You must be willing to be vulnerable and truthful throughout the discovery process. It's the truth that will set you free. Dedicate yourself to prayerfully considering and then diligently trying the suggestions that are offered to you.

Some of the counselor's recommendations may seem ridiculous because they're so counterintuitive or countercultural. Have a heart of faith that the time-tested, sacred solutions presented in God's Word can bring about transformational change. God is the incomparable great I AM who is able to do exceedingly abundantly above all that we could ever ask or think according to the power that works in us (Ephesians 3:20).

Yes, God is able to help you do all things through Christ, who strengthens you. But it will take time to disengage from difficulties and detangle the knotty places in your life. The chaos and confusion adversely impacting anyone's life typically evolve over time, and what we must all realize is that God needs time to mitigate our mistakes and work wonderfully to accomplish His ultimate purposes in our lives. A favorite quote shared by a friend of mine many years ago, one that I hope will encourage your heart, is, "What unfolds slowly unfolds surely." Truth be told, it may take years of painstaking work before your situation is remedied according to God's plan. God is not in a frantic hurry as we are. Just as the farmer works hard cultivating the ground, planting the seed into the ground, and then watering the ground before reaping a plentiful harvest, we must put in the hard work to obtain a harvest of blessings in our lives. Through it all, we'll learn the valuable life lessons our Master Teacher wants to teach us when our hearts are receptive, and we do things God's way.

Pay attention to the advice given in Proverbs 3: 5-8 (LB), "...trust the Lord completely; don't ever trust yourself. In everything you do, put God first, and he will direct you and crown your efforts with success. Don't be conceited, sure of your own wisdom. Instead, trust and reverence the Lord, and turn your back on evil; when you do that, then you will be given renewed health and vitality." It's obvious that there will be work for you to do if you're going to derive God's blessings. Correcting problems and stabilizing your situation will probably not come easily. You can't blink your eyes or click your heels three times and be catapulted to a place of peace. You must work tirelessly with intentionality day in and day out to achieve the righteous results that bring great joy. Part of the work entails turning your back on evil. We're reminded of that in 1 Peter 3:11, where it states that we should turn away from evil and do good, seek peace, and pursue it. You'll have to actively turn away from any people, places, and things that drag you down into life-threatening quicksand. Get rid of the evildoers, haters, and naysayers in your life, and keep company with like-minded folks who believe in God and believe in you and the great plans God has for your life. It's your job to cultivate a network of supporters who provide God-guided protection and provision that's helpful to you in bad times and in good times.

Expect that there will be days you'll falter or even fail miserably, related to your improvement strategies. Stay encouraged because a statement by Dr. Mary McLeod Bethune, famous educator and civil rights activist, bears repeating: "Neither God nor man can use a discouraged soul." Wipe the dust off your feet and start all over again. Failures are the stepping stones to future successes. You can control your responses to setbacks, so don't let them become stumbling blocks. Think impetus, not impediment. What comes your way can be the impetus for you to do better and be better when you try to see that what's happening is only a temporary impediment. Remember this: things come to pass, not to stay!

Wise counsel or sound advice is something we should all be seeking as we move forward in life. Guidance from godly sources keeps us on track or helps us get back on track, so we're moving in a divine direction. You can't go wrong when you remember what God says about Himself and the help He provides, as stated in Proverbs 8:14 and 17 (ESV), "I have counsel and sound wisdom; I have insight; I have strength… I love those who love me, and those who seek me diligently find me."

Chapter 6, Biblical Behavior Modification, was devoted to presenting five God-approved methods to help bring about changes in behavior so there is better alignment with God's standards. As we align ourselves to the Lord's standards, our lives produce outstanding outcomes, a cornucopia of bountiful blessings as God operates on our behalf. As you thoughtfully and judiciously engage in prayer, instruction, encouragement, correction, and counseling throughout the parenting process, you'll emerge a stronger parent who is better equipped to build secure, capable, joyful children as they move through the various stages of their growth and development. You'll be helping your children grow up to be image-bearers of God who can navigate the world they live in, making a divine difference in His precious name.

SEVEN

Pursue Excellence

> *"Look carefully then how you walk, not as unwise but as wise, making the best use of time, because the days are evil. Therefore, do not be foolish, but understand what the will of the Lord is." Ephesians 5:15-17(ESV)*

No one can dispute the fact that the days we're living in are evil. There are wars raging on multiple fronts. Leaders in government, various industries, and even in the church seem to be trying to outdo each other for power, prestige, and wealth. Criminals escape punishment while innocent people spend years behind bars. Scammers and con artists are ripping off unsuspecting people on a daily basis. I could cite other examples of evil, but you get the point. We're living in some dark and demanding times. If there ever was a time for Christians to be guided by eternal truth as we walk in the light of Christ, it's now. The truth is, we are the light this dark world desperately needs. Christian parents must steadfastly walk in the light of Christ's love, firmly holding onto His unfailing promises. How critical it is for Christian parents and other concerned adults in the Body of Christ to resist the mediocrity that's so prevalent today. All Christians must be ever mindful of their witness to children. We are training up the next generation, the young people who'll need to play a pivotal role for the cause of Christ.

The adults who are entrusted with the growth and development of children must be careful to reflect God's love and rely on the Holy

Spirit where our children are concerned. The Scriptural mandate is clear: we are to train our children in the way they should go. May God grant us wise and discerning minds and compassionate hearts as we endeavor to live up to this awesome responsibility and privilege. Psalm 90:12 (ESV) states, "So teach us to number our days that we may get a heart of wisdom."

Focusing on the brevity of time to make an indelible mark on a child's life is likely the furthest thing from a parent's mind when a baby comes home from the hospital. Those first days are very daunting. But consider this: if the child you cradle and caress as an infant goes off to college at age 18, you have a mere 6,574 days to make an impression on your child's life in meaningful ways, and those precious few days are further diminished by the facts of life. Children spend time sleeping, going to school, attending play dates and summer camp, visiting grandparents' houses, participating in sports and music practices, and on and on it goes. If you add up all the hours that your children are not in your direct care, the time to build your parental legacy is much shorter than you think. We all waste a certain amount of time. But when it comes to parenting, there's no time to lose. The Lord advised the Israelites to be mindful of using time and opportunities to their full advantage when interacting with children. Speaking of God's laws in Deuteronomy 6:6,7 (CEV), we see, "Memorize his laws and tell them to your children over and over again. Talk about them all the time, whether you're at home or walking along the road or going to bed at night, or getting up in the morning." What these verses say to me is that being intentional and strategic on a daily basis is of utmost importance.

What do I mean by being intentional and strategic? Let's explore the definitions of both words. According to Webster's New World Dictionary, the word intentional means done purposely. Well, while that sounds simple enough, you'll find it tough to do things purposely as the rigors of life come into play and oftentimes get in the way. However, you must not lose sight of your purpose as a

Christian parent, and that is to help your child come to saving faith in Jesus Christ and then nurture your child's faith as the years go on. Without God's help on a daily basis, it will be an impossible task to do things purposefully. So, what does strategic mean? A strategic approach to living means you're applying skills in planning and managing activities to achieve your goals. Without purposeful planning on your part, it's easy to fritter away the precious few days you have to train your children in the way they should go. Christian parents must fight with all their might to manage time wisely to avoid being engaged in activities that do little to build secure, joyful children who are strong in faith and good works.

Three of the basic principles of time management are: **prioritize, organize, and concentrate.** The things that are important to God are clearly presented in His Word. These are the things that should be important to you. The world will pummel you with its priorities, things like obtaining wealth and power, and prestige. The Lord wants us to become more and more like our Savior, Jesus Christ.

Developing godly character in ourselves and our children is the first order of business. You must be willing to put in the hard work to operate with Christ-honoring integrity in every facet of your life. As Christ states in John 15:5, "...for apart from me you can do nothing." Prioritize your parental efforts, so you're actively engaging in the work that builds your child's life on the firm foundation of Jesus Christ.

It's advantageous to find out where you're doing well as a parent and where you're faltering. Something to consider is to partner with your spouse or another trusted person who can provide perspective whenever you embark on an evaluative phase of your parenting journey. Collaboration strengthens bonds of connectedness and helps each person, crucial to the parenting process, hone vital skills. Use a parent assessment tool. A more formal assessment will enable you to identify and prioritize your weaknesses, as well as highlight your strengths. Once you've identified your strengths and weaknesses, hold fast to your strengths and eliminate your weaknesses little by little. You and your children will be glad you did. I recommend you go to preachitteachit.org/archives/5115[1], to view *Twelve Self-Assessment Questions for Christian Parents*, along with a seven-point *Plan for Growth in Grace*. Content is briefly presented below to whet your appetite related to identifying how you're doing as a parent:

Assessment Questions

1. Is the Christian faith a regular part of our daily conversation?
2. Do I offer regular opportunities for my children to worship God?
3. Does my speech serve the purpose of building up my children?
4. Am I teaching obedience by modeling it and requiring it?
5. Do I demonstrate the fruit of the Spirit in my life and in my parenting?
6. Do I avoid exasperating my children with standards that are too high?
7. Does my conduct towards my children reflect love?
8. Do I pray for my children and trust God with them, enabling me to live free of worry about them?
9. Have I put away anger?
10. Is my discipline corrective instead of punitive?
11. Do I point my children toward the gospel when they sin?
12. Do I view my children as blessings from God?

Growth Plan

1. Focus on YOUR relationship with God.
2. Confess sin to God, AND your children, when appropriate.
3. Receive God's forgiveness.

4. Go to God daily (and sometimes hourly) for grace and wisdom.
5. Focus on one area of growth at a time.
6. Memorize Scripture.
7. Enlist the help of others.

As you can see, this article, written by Luke and Trisha Gilkerson, provides a substantive tool to ensure you're doing the things you can do to move in the right direction. It provides a roadmap to help you stay on course as it relates to your parenting. Check out the article in its entirety. It absolutely warrants a deeper dive if you're serious about improving your parenting skills. When it comes to focusing on one area of growth at a time, something that's absolutely essential to do, you can summon up enough courage to ask older children this question: If you could name one thing you think would help me to be a better parent, what would that be? Be willing to listen and then prayerfully consider how to improve in that crucial area. Think about the dramatic impact that one act of humility and determination to improve your parenting could have on your children.

It's critical to prayerfully **prioritize** your parental efforts to get you going in the right direction and then **organize** yourself and **concentrate** on the useful activities that help you stay the course, so you keep going in the right direction. People in the business community use a tool called a strategic plan to direct their efforts so that they achieve corporate goals. Without being overly complex or formal, your family can benefit from strategic planning. Strategic plans help businesses allocate resources, energy, and assets. The primary goal of a strategic plan is to formalize efforts so that all stakeholders are on the same page and striving to reach the same end results. Isn't being on the same page and striving to reach the same goals something your family can benefit from? Creating a family strategic plan requires a disciplined effort, but the process is well worth the time and effort.

If you took the recommendation to complete a parent assessment to identify and prioritize your weaknesses, you are already on your way in the planning process. It's always important to honestly and objectively assess your strengths and weaknesses. Also, make sure you look at current opportunities, complexities, and threats to your family's security and stability, things like a move to another state or the loss of a loved one or a job. You'll want to have a clear picture of what you're up against so you can pinpoint the wisest use of your assets on a day-to-day basis. Create a mission statement for your family and list a few objectives. This ensures everyone is focused on the same goal. Your mission statement and objectives might be something like:

Mission Statement

To help the children adjust to the sudden loss of their grandfather after his massive heart attack.

Objectives

- To pray with and for the children regarding their loss.
- To provide opportunities for everyone in the family to share their feelings about the loss.
- To read a children's book about grief.
- To watch a children's video about grief.
- To encourage the children to talk, write about, and/or draw pictures about their "true" feelings.
- To check out and possibly join the grief share support group that meets once a month at the church.
- To take the children to one of Grandpa's favorite spots to share special memories.
- To host a family and friends "I Remember Grandpa" gathering, which includes his favorite foods & desserts, music, activities, or a trivia contest.

- To enlist the children's help in putting together a celebratory scrapbook honoring their grandpa.

Designate who will be responsible for certain aspects of the plan. Jot down the resources you'll need to achieve the listed objectives. An example of that might be:

Needed Resources
- Bible passages, devotional materials about grief.
- Children's books and videos about grief.
- Art supplies.
- Details about dates and times of future grief share meetings.
- Money and time to revisit one of Grandpa's favorite places.
- Family members and friends to help plan, organize, and implement the "I Remember Grandpa" event.
- Scrapbooking examples, materials, and time to work on the project.

When you know what you're trying to achieve and who is responsible for each goal, then it's time to deploy your plan and measure your progress along the way. Weekly family meetings will help you gain important feedback to determine if you're headed in the right direction. If not, don't be afraid to revise your plan accordingly. Once you achieve several objectives, regroup and set new objectives. Keep setting goals that continually move your family forward on the paths God wants you to travel.

What bumpy roads are you currently traveling on, or what dangerous waters are you swimming in? How fast are you speeding down those roads or quickly sinking in the perilous waters? Is your life currently a blur or quickly becoming one as you whiz from activity to activity? Are you spinning out of control or drowning? Do you feel like the Internet is consuming far too much of your time or your children's time? In his book The Shallows, Nicholas Carr describes how the Internet has shaped our relationship with stillness: "What the Net seems to be doing is chipping away my capacity for concentration and contemplation. Whether I'm online or not, my mind now expects to take in information the way the Net distributes it: in a swiftly moving stream of particles..."[2] Does Carr's quote evoke a hearty amen from you?

Before you conclude this final chapter of *A Blueprint For Building Children: Following God's Plan*, I encourage you to take one last **SELAH** moment. Sit in stillness and quiet contemplation before God. There is a lesser-known hymn called *Wash, O God, Our Sons, and Daughters* that I hope you'll take a few minutes to listen to in a deliberate moment of solitude. Let the words of the hymn settle into your soul. There are a number of different arrangements of the song presented on YouTube, but my personal favorite is by Oleta Adams. Listen to the arrangement that appeals to you. After you listen to the song, and I'm providing the lyrics for you, sit silently before God and take in how the song speaks to your heart.

In your stillness and silence before God, as you listen intently, I pray you'll receive prompting, instruction, or encouragement from the Lord.

Wash, O God, Our Sons, And Daughters[3]

Wash, O God, our sons, and daughters,
Where Your cleansing waters flow.
Number them among Your people;
Bless as Christ blessed long ago.
Weave them garments bright and sparkling;
Compass them with love and light.
Fill, anoint them; Send Your Spirit,
Holy Dove and heart's delight.

We who bring them long for nurture;
By Your milk may we be fed.
Let us join your feast, partaking
Cup of blessing, living bread.
God, renew us, Guide our footsteps;
Free from sin and all its snares,
One with Christ
In living, dying,
By Your Spirit, children, heirs.

O, how deep Your holy wisdom!
Unimagined, all Your ways!
To Your name be glory, honor!
With our lives, we worship praise!
We, Your people, stand before You,
Water-washed and Spirit-born.
By Your grace, our lives we offer
Recreate us; God transform!

Whether you listened to your preferred musical arrangement of Wash, O God, Our Sons, and Daughters or not, you can read in the last line this phrase, Recreate us, God, transform! The only way you'll be recreated and transformed into the parent God wants you to be and your children need you to be is by the renewing of your mind. That happens when you saturate your mind with Scripture, walk by faith and not by sight, and let Christ's example of limitless and unconditional love be your righteous role model. As you interact with your children day in and day out, **PURSUE excellence** as if your children's lives depend on it because that's the case! Perhaps the refrain from New Covenant Christian Academy's original school song will resonate with you. Maybe some of the lyrics sung by students and staff at my now-closed Christian school can live on in your home. The words were, "We are striving for excellence, excellence in His name, working together for wonderful results." Think about and recite that refrain frequently as a mantra. You can't raise your children alone. You need Christ's help and the help of other godly influencers to bring about the wonderful results that every parent seeks to see in their children's lives. You must actively pursue excellence because the riptide of mediocre parenting is strong and relentless, drowning countless families in the troubled waters of today's challenging times. Christ is your unfailing Life Preserver, the One who'll come to your rescue every single time.

No matter how much of a mess you think your parenting has been to this point, it's never too late to reboot. Do not be enslaved by guilt and pain from past mistakes as though you were a shackled prisoner lugging around a ball and chain. In Christ, you're free to pursue a different path. "Stand fast therefore in the liberty by which Christ has made us free, and do not be entangled again with a yoke of bondage" (Galatians 5:1). Take what continues to disturb you and place those mistakes under your feet, using them as the stepping stones that elevate you to future parenting successes. Parenting is a marathon and not a sprint. Parent with the finish line in the forefront of your mind. As you raise your children with godly intentionality, you can expect a generational legacy like the one depicted in Psalm 78:5-7 (ESV) which says, "He established a testimony in Jacob and appointed a law in Israel, which he commanded our fathers to teach their children, that the next generation might know them, the children yet unborn, and arise and tell them to their children, so that they should set their hope in God and not forget the works of God, but keep his commandments;" Don't you want your parental testimony to be the main conduit that motivates your children to put their hope in God?

Place your trust in a totally trustworthy God, the One who is who He says He is, the One whose character doesn't change, and the One whose promises never fail. God is your power source, but you must tap into His limitless power day in and day out. You probably have seen a power strip that allows four or more devices to be plugged into it. If the main plug of the power strip is inserted into one of the outlets on the strip itself, there is no power flowing through it, rendering it useless. You can plug your devices into the remaining outlets on the strip, and the result is the same...no power. So just as that power strip must draw power from an external outlet, its source of power, so we must not rely on ourselves, but draw power from the **Source**, our almighty and powerful God. The Lord has the power available for you to parent in ways that are unique and specially designed to help you guide your children in the ways that help them fulfill God's intended purpose for them. Do not be fearful that godly parenting will alienate your children. As it says in Proverbs 3:5&6 (ESV), "Trust in the Lord with all your heart, and do not lean on your own understanding. In all your ways acknowledge him, and he will make straight your paths." What you need to do is to lead your children on straight paths, and God will help you do that. Your steadfast, loving, godly parenting will not alienate your children; it will endear you to them. Though a fictional character in the *Manga* series, *Demon Slayer: Kimetsu no Yaiba*, Tanjiro Komado provided food for thought for today's parents when he said, "How your children treat you when they're no longer obligated to listen to you is a direct reflection of your parenting skills and the impact you had on them as a human."

Do you want to have the greatest impact on your children that's humanly possible? The answer to that question is easy. The day-to-day choices that bring about lasting, impactful results that honor God and cultivate your children's respect for you won't always be easy, especially when it's easier to get caught up in the dizzying pace that entraps many parents. Expect the choices to be very difficult on many occasions. But don't be afraid to make the difficult choices that God wants you to make because He's got your back. Remember, parenting children is sacred work that God will bless abundantly when you intentionally choose to build your house on the firm foundation of Jesus Christ and not on the shaky foundation of current parenting trends. **Pursue excellence** as you follow Jesus Christ, the One who has had the greatest impact on human history. He'll lead you in every facet of your parenting so you can have an impact on your children's lives that's far above anything you could ever fathom. God has the blueprint for building children. Follow His plan.

Appendices

Appendix A
Salvation

A Blueprint For Building Children: Following God's Plan presents material designed to help Christian parents, grandparents, caregivers, teachers, and others in the "village" who help to train children in the way they should go. If you're not sure you are a Christian (someone who relies on Jesus Christ's atoning work on Calvary to save them from an eternity separated from God), the simple plan of Salvation follows:

Plan of Salvation

1. Admit your need (I am a sinner) - Romans 3:23 (NIV) - "For all have sinned and fall short of the glory of God."

2. Turn from your sins (repent)– Acts 3:19 (NIV) - "Repent, then, and turn to God, so that your sins may be wiped out, that times of refreshing may come from the Lord,"

3. Believe that Jesus Christ died to take away your sins - John 3:16 (NIV) - "For God so loved the world that he gave his one and only Son, that whoever believes in him shall not perish but have eternal life." 1 John 4:9 (NIV) - "This is how God showed his love among us; He sent his one and only son into the world that we might live through him." Romans 5:8 (NIV) - "But God demonstrates his own love for us in this; While we were still sinners, Christ died for us."

4. Invite Jesus Christ to come into your heart and control your life -Romans 10:9,13 (NIV) - "If you declare with your mouth,

'Jesus is Lord,' and believe in your heart that God raised him from the dead, you will be saved... for, 'Everyone who calls on the name of the Lord will be saved.'"

Lift the following or a similar prayer to the Lord, believing by faith that He hears your heart cry and saves you:

Dear Lord,

I know I am a sinner. I believe that Jesus Christ died on the cross for my sins and rose from the dead. I now repent of my sin and invite Jesus into my life. Thank You, Jesus, for shedding Your precious blood so that I might have the free gift of eternal life. Lord, thank You for the Holy Spirit and Your infallible Word to guide me from this day forward. Help me to love You and live for You.

In Jesus' name, I pray. Amen.

Appendix B
Poetry

This section presents poems for your consideration, selections that can be read, recited, and memorized. According to Webster's New World Dictionary, poems are an arrangement of words, especially a rhythmical composition, sometimes rhymed, in a style more imaginative than ordinary speech or prose. There is enormous benefit in reading, reciting, memorizing, and writing poetry.

Poetry is a testament to the power, strength, encouragement, solace, and inspiration that we can receive as we delve into the author's musings on a given subject.

Research shows that poetry reading, writing, speaking, and memorizing can support our mental health, especially in times of turmoil or great need. A 2021 study of hospitalized children found that providing opportunities for them to read and write poetry reduced their fear, sadness, anger, worry, and fatigue. Oftentimes, a poem will stir our souls and linger in our minds long after something else we've read on the subject fades away.

Poet Janice Haer and I hope the poems included in Appendix B will be used mightily by God in unique and creative ways to bless your family and provide a springboard to explore further the many benefits poetry can have in your life.

Poems By J. S. Haer - Character Is The Key

Poems By J. S. Haer - Character Is The Key

OBEDIENCE

God spoke to Noah and said to him, "Build an ark."
Noah listened to God. And he obeyed God.
Although it made no sense.

God spoke to Abraham and said to him, "Take your son to be sacrificed."
Abraham listened to God. And he obeyed God.
Although it made no sense.

God spoke to Joshua and said to him, "March around the walls of
Jericho."
Joshua listened to God. And he obeyed God.
Although it made no sense.

Noah. Abraham. Joshua.
All heard God.

All listened to God. All obeyed God.
Although it made no sense.

God speaks to you,
a precious child of His, and says to you,
"Children, obey your parents in all things,
for this is well pleasing unto God."

Listen. Trust. Obey.
Although it makes no sense.
Listen. Trust. Obey.
"For this is pleasing unto God."
Listen. Trust. Obey.
"For this is pleasing. Unto God."
Colossians 3:20

REVERENCE

What a strange sight,
Moses must have thought.
A bush on fire
but not burning up.

What a strange voice,
Moses must have thought.
A voice speaking
but no one was around.

What a strange message,
Moses must have thought.
God saying, "Do not come any closer.
Take off your sandals, because
you are standing on holy ground."

What special words.
Moses must have thought.
"This must be a special place for
I am standing on holy ground.
I am standing on HOLY GROUND!"

Special words.
Special place.
Moses must have thought.

So, Moses must have said,
"I will always treat God with all my love."
"I will always treat God. With all my love!"
Exodus 3:5

WISDOM

Two men.
One foolish. One wise.

Two houses. One built
by a foolish, foolish man.
On the shifting, shifting sand.

Two houses. One built
by a very wise, wise man.
On a solid rock.

Rains came. Floods came.
Winds blew. Winds beat.
On the house on the shifting sand.
On the house on the solid rock.

What happened to that house
of the foolish, foolish man?
It went crashing, crashing down!

What happened to that house
of the very wise, wise man?
It didn't go crashing, crashing down!

And what did Jesus teach
about that foolish, foolish man?
A house built on shifting sand
can never, never ever stand.

And what did Jesus teach
about that very wise, wise man?
Always, always do
what God has taught you to.
Always, always do
what God has taught you to.

Then Jesus said to everyone,
"Anyone who hears and obeys
these teachings of mine
is like a wise person
who built a house
on solid rock."

Like a wise person
who built a house
on solid rock.
Like a wise person.
Who built a house.
On solid rock.
Matthew 7:24 CEV

FAITH

Faith is
knowing.
God loves you.
All the time.
Even though you
cannot hear Him
cannot see Him
cannot touch Him.

Faith is
knowing.
God's love is with you.
Everywhere.
Even though you
cannot hear Him
cannot see Him
cannot touch Him.

Faith is
knowing.
God's love surrounds you.
All the time
and everywhere.
Even though you
cannot hear Him
cannot see Him
cannot touch Him.

Faith is

knowing.

Knowing faith will

grow and grow and grow.

Then, big things will happen.

If you remember the words of Jesus.

"…if you have faith

the size of a mustard seed,

you could say to this mountain,

'Go from here to there,

and it will go'…"

Say to this mountain.

Go from here to there.

And it will go.

And. It will. Go.

Matthew 17:20 CEB

HONESTY

Adam knew.
Eve knew.
DO NOT EAT!
Do not eat
the forbidden fruit.
Growing on THAT tree.
In the middle of the garden.
DO NOT EAT!

But Eve ate.
Then Adam ate.
And God knew.
God knew!
God cannot be fooled.
God cannot be fooled!

First Eve lied to God.
The serpent made me do it.
The serpent made me do it!

Then Adam lied to God.
That woman made me do it.
That woman made me do it!

Didn't Eve know she lied to God?
Of course she did. Of course she did!

Didn't Adam know he lied to God?
Of course he did. Of course he did!

God cannot be fooled.
God cannot be fooled!
God shows us how.
To always tell the truth.
God shows us how.
To always act in honesty.

God gives us all
His one and only Son
His Son Jesus who said,
"I am the way, the truth, and the life."
"I am the way, the truth, and the life."

Look to Jesus.
Listen to Jesus.
Follow Jesus.
He is the Way.
He is the Truth.
He is the Life.
The Way.
The Truth.
The Life.
John 14:6

PATIENCE

Abraham and Sarah.
Loved children.
Very much.
But they had none.
None of their own.
None of their own.

One day God spoke to Abraham.
"Someday I'll give you a son.
And your son's
children's children's children
will have many, many more children. More children
than all the stars in heaven.
Than all the stars in heaven."

So, Abraham and Sarah waited.
Waited for 1 year, 2 years, 3 years.
Then 4 years, 5 years, 6 years.
And 7, 8, 9 years.
10, 11, 12 years.
13, 14, 15 years.
16, 17, 18 years.
19, 20, 21 years.
22, 23, 24 years.
24 years?

Then it happened.
Then it happened!
Year 25 came!

Abraham and Sarah had a son.
Abraham and Sarah had a son!
And they named him Isaac.

Waiting 25 years.
Was a very long time.
Waiting 25 years.
Was very hard to do.

Waiting 25 years.
Waiting 25 months.
Waiting 25 weeks.
Waiting 25 days.

Waiting is very hard to do.
Very hard to do!

But God can help you wait.
God can help you wait.
Long ago He said,
"Rest in the Lord,
and wait patiently for him."

"Rest in the Lord.
Wait patiently for him."
Rest. In the Lord.
Wait. Patiently for him.
Rest. Wait. Patiently.
Psalm 37:7a KJV

THANKFULNESS

Daniel loved God.
God loved Daniel.

Daniel was a Jew.
Who lived in Jerusalem.
And he worshipped God.
Everyday.

One day. After a war.
Daniel and other Jews.
Were taken away.
Taken away. To live in another land.
Another land. A faraway land.
Called Babylon.

Even though Daniel lived.
In a far away land. He
continued to pray.
Everyday.
Always, always giving thanks.
Thanks to God.
Three times a day.
Three times a day!

One day.
The King of Babylon.
Made a law.
Made a law that said.
Everyone must pray.
To him. The King of Babylon.
To him. The King of Babylon!

Disobey the law?
You'll be thrown in. To a lion's den.
You'll be thrown in. To a lion's den!
Daniel continued to pray.
Everyday.
Always giving thanks.
Always giving thanks.
It did not matter.
He could be thrown. To the lions.
He could be thrown. To the lions!

But Daniel was caught.
Caught praying to his God.
And not. To the King of Babylon.
And not. To the King of Babylon!
The King of Babylon
was sad. Very sad.
He liked Daniel. Very much.
But he had to throw Daniel in.
Throw him. In the lion's den.
Throw him. In the lion's den!
For a law is a law.
And must be obeyed.
And must be obeyed!

But the Lord God.
Shut up the mouths.
Of the lions.
And not one lion. Touched Daniel.
And not one lion. Touched Daniel!
He did not die. He did not die!

Daniel had never stopped praying.
Never stopped giving thanks.
Even when. It was against the law.
Even when. It was against the law!

Was Daniel taught?
Did Daniel always know?
"In everything give thanks.
For this is God's will for you."

We can live a life.
Like Daniel.
Always giving thanks.
"For this is God's will for you.
In everything give thanks."
In everything. Give thanks.
In everything. Give. Thanks.
1 Thessalonians 5:18 NET

SELF-CONTROL

Saul was king.
King of Israel.
David was an army commander.
For the King of Israel.
One day
King Saul
got an idea.
A bad idea.
A very bad idea.
King Saul thought.
"I think David
wants to become king."
This cannot happen.
This cannot happen!

So, King Saul made a plan. (A bad plan).
A very bad plan.
My men and I
will hunt David.
When we find him.
We will take his life.
We will take his life!
So, the hunt began.
David and his men.
Running and fleeing.
Running and fleeing!
All over Israel.
All over Israel!

So, the hunt began.
King Saul and his men.
Running and chasing.
Running and chasing.
All over Israel.
All over Israel!

One day
David and his men found.
A deep, dark cave.
A deep, dark cave! They all went in.
They all hid.
And they could not be seen.
And they could not be seen!

Saul happened to come by.
But he could not see.
David and his men.
Hiding in the cave.
He could not see.
David and his men.
Hiding in the cave.
Saul went in.
All alone.
A perfect time.
For David to take.
The life of his king.
The life of his king!
But David could not.
But David could not!
Take the life of his king.
Take the life of his king!

David's men were surprised.
And they whispered to David.
"Now is your chance."
"Now is your chance."
"Take the life of the king."
"Take the life of the king!"

Still,

David could not take.
David could not take!
The life of his king.
The life of his king!
David did not do.
What perhaps he wanted to do.
Because he stopped.
And thought.
Because he stopped!
And thought!

I cannot do.
What is wrong.
I cannot do!
What is wrong!
David did not do.
What his men wanted him to do.
Because he stopped.
And thought.
Because he stopped!
And thought! I cannot do.
What is wrong.
I cannot do!
What is wrong!

Always. Remember.
Stop. Think.
Stop! Think!
"Better a patient person
than a warrior,
one with self-control
than one who takes the city."
Better a patient person…
one with self-control.
Better a patient person…
one with self-control.
One. With. Self-control.
Proverbs 25:28 NLT

TENDERHEARTEDNESS

A long time ago.
A long, long time ago.
There were two groups.
Of people.
Who did not.
Like each other.
One tiny bit.
Not even one tiny bit.
The Jews.
Did not like.
The Samaritans.
Absolutely not!
The Samaritans.
Did not like the Jews.
Absolutely not!

One day
a man was walking.
All alone.
In his own country.
Of Israel.
Some robbers spotted him.
And decided to rob him.
Beat him.
Take most of his clothes.
Then leave him.
At the side of the road.
Barely alive.
Barely alive!

This man.
Barely alive.
Needed help.
Needed help!
And fast.
Very fast!

A Jewish leader
came along.
Took one look.
At the barely alive man.
And passed by.
On the other side.
Of the road.
On the other side.
Of the road!
Another Jewish leader
came along.
Took one look.
At the barely alive man.
And passed by.
On the other side.
Of the road.
On the other side.
Of the road!
One more man
came along.
He was not.
A Jewish leader.
He was.
A Samaritan man.
He was.
A Samaritan man!

Took one look.
At the barely alive man.
And said.
I've got to help this man.
I've got to help this man!
It does not matter.
I am a Samaritan.
He needs help.
Very fast.
He needs help!
Very fast!

So this Samaritan man this
Good Samaritan man.
Stopped. And took care of
This injured Jewish man.
This injured Jewish man.

The injured Jewish man
needed time to rest.
Needed time to heal.
So, the Good Samaritan man
put the injured man.
On his donkey.
And took him to
An inn.
And paid for him.
To stay there.
Until he healed.
Until he healed!

An injured man.
A Good Samaritan.
A Good Samaritan who
knew in his heart.
…"be kind to one another,
tenderhearted,
forgiving one another
as God in Christ has
forgiven you."
A Good Samaritan
who knew in his heart.
Be kind. To one another.
Be tenderhearted. To one another.
Be forgiving. To one another.
Be kind. Be tenderhearted. Be forgiving.
Be…
kind, tenderhearted, forgiving.
Kind. Tenderhearted. Forgiving.
Ephesians 4:32 NRSV

ORDERLINESS

God had a job.
A big job.
A very big job.
For a man.
Named Noah.

God asked Noah.
Could you build me?
An ark?
A very big ark?
And after you build it.
Could you take?
Take 2 of every
living creature?
Take 2 of every
living creature?
And…your family too.
And…your family too!
You see.
There's going to be.
A flood!
A big flood! A very big flood!
The ark will keep. All the animals safe.
And your family too.
And your family too!
I'll tell you, Noah.
Exactly what to do.
Exactly what to do!

I'll tell you.
What kind of wood to use.
I'll tell you.
How long. How wide. How high.
The ark will need to be.
When the ark is done.
All done.
I'll tell you.
How to load.
All the animals.
In the proper order.
Can't have those elephants.
Stepping on.
Those creepy, crawly creatures.
Stepping on.
Those creepy crawly creatures!

Noah did.
Everything in order.
Just as God had said.
Then it was time.
Time to shut the door.
Time to shut the door!
And let the rains begin.
And let the rains begin!
The rains began.
Dropping. Dropping. Dropping.
Day after day.
Night after night.

Forty days.

Forty nights.

Forty days and forty nights.

Forty days and forty nights!

It rained and rained and rained.

It rained and rained and rained!

The rains. Finally.

Stopped dropping.

The flood. Finally.

Dried up.

All the animals.

Were safe.

All the animals.

Were safe!

And the family too.

And the family too!

Noah did.

Exactly what. God had asked.

Step by step.

One thing.

After the other.

All in order.

All in order!

For God knew then.

God knows now.

To..."let all things be done

decently and in order." Let

all things.

Be done.

Decently.

In order.

Decently.

In. Order.

1 Corinthians 14:40 KJV

PURITY

Jesus.
Was a teacher.
A great teacher.
But. He did not teach.
Inside a classroom.
But. He did not teach.
Inside a classroom!
Every place and any place.
Was His classroom.
Small spaces. Big spaces.
Big spaces. Small spaces.
Every place and any place.
Was His classroom.

People came.
From all over.
Near and far.
Far and near.
Just to hear.
Jesus teach.
Just to hear.
Jesus teach!

People came.
Young ones. Old ones.
Old ones. Young ones.
Just to hear.
Jesus teach.
Just to hear.
Jesus teach!

People came.
In small groups. Big groups.
In big groups. Small groups.
Just to hear.
Jesus teach.
Just to hear.
Jesus teach!

Jesus taught.
Sometimes telling stories.
Telling stories. You know and love.
Easy to learn.
Easy to remember.
Easy to learn.
Easy to remember!
Jesus taught.
Sometimes saying only.
A few short words.
Easy to learn.
Easy to remember.
Easy to learn.
Easy to remember!

Jesus taught.
Sometimes stories.
Sometimes only a few short words.
To help us learn.
To help us remember.
To help us feel.
How God. Is always with us.
In our hearts.
Every day.
Everywhere.

Every day!
Everywhere!
Jesus taught us.
When we keep God.
Only God.
In our hearts.
We will be blessed.
We will be happy.
For He said...
"Happy are people
who have pure hearts,
because they will
see God."
"Happy are people
who have pure hearts,
because they will
see God."

Jesus taught us.
Have room in your heart.
Only for God.
Have room.
In your heart.
Only for God.
And you will. See God.
You will. See. God.
Matthew 5:18 CEB

FORGIVENESS

When Joseph

was a young

boy.

All his older brothers thought.

JOSEPH IS A PEST!

A REALLY BIG PEST!

He was always having.

Strange dreams.

Really strange dreams. Like.

One day his brothers would.

All bow down.

To their youngest brother Joseph.

And they did not like.

That thought at all.

And they did not like.

That thought at all!

Joseph also had.

A special coat. A beautiful coat.

None of the brothers had.

A special coat. A beautiful coat.

Like Joseph had.

Dreams and a special coat.

A special coat and dreams.

None of the brothers.

Liked Joseph at all.

For these reasons.

They had to do something.

They had to do something!

One day.
Joseph went to the fields.
Where all his brothers.
Were watching.
The family flock of sheep.
The brothers got an idea.
A bad idea.
A very bad idea.
A very terrible bad idea.
A group of men.
Were traveling to Egypt.
The brothers decided.
Let's sell Joseph.
To these travelers.
On their way to Egypt.
On their way to Egypt!
And they did.
And they did!
Joseph lived in Egypt. For many, many years.

The King of Egypt.
Started having.
Strange dreams.
Very strange dreams.
No one in all of Egypt.
Could tell the King.
The meaning of his dreams.
But someone knew.
Joseph could tell.
The meaning of dreams.
And he could tell.
The King of Egypt.
The meaning of his dreams.

The meaning of his dreams!

Joseph did know.
Know the exact meaning.
Of the dreams.
The King was having.
Joseph told the King
For seven years.
You will have.
Plenty of food to eat.
Then for seven years.
You won't have enough.
Enough food. To eat.
You won't have enough.
Enough food to eat!

Joseph also had a plan.
A plan to have.
Enough to eat.
Even when. The food would run out.
The King liked Joseph's plan.
Save food. In the seven good years.
And you will have. Enough to eat.
In the next seven years.
And that is what.
Joseph did.
And no one went hungry.
In all the land of Egypt.
In all the land of Egypt!

But in the land
where Joseph was born.
His brothers. His father.

All were starving.
All were
starving!
They heard about
the extra food.
In the land of Egypt.
So Joseph's father Jacob
decided to send.
The 10 older brothers.
Down to Egypt.
To buy some extra food.
To buy some extra food!

When the 10 brothers
got to Egypt.
They did not.
Recognize Joseph. At all.
But Joseph recognized.
All 10 brothers.
All 10 brothers!

He did not tell
all his brothers.
Who he was.
Who he was!
He gave them food.
Told them to come back.
This time with their father.
And their younger brother Benjamin.
So the whole family.
Came down to Egypt.
This time
Joseph told them.

Who he was.
Who he was!

Then Joseph did.
Something you won't believe.
Something you won't believe!
Right then.
Right there.
On the spot.
He forgave them.
For what they did to him.
For what they did to him!
Joseph had been treated.
Badly. Very badly.
By his 10 older brothers.

Somehow.
Somehow he was able.
Able to...
"Judge not and
you shall not be judged.
Condemn not and
you shall not be condemned.
Forgive, and you will be forgiven."

Judge not.
Condemn not.
Forgive.
Forgive. And
you will be forgiven
Forgive.
You. Will be. Forgiven.
Luke 6:37

JANICE SPRAGUE HAER fell in love with God at the age of four and a half when she attended her first Daily Vacation Bible School and saw Bible stories come to life as the teacher put each flannel character on the flannel board. At the age of twelve, she began serving God by playing the piano for Sunday School and Evening Youth Fellowship worship services. Blessed with the gift of music, Janice obtained her music education degree, and for over 55 years, she taught children from preschool to sixth grade. In 2018, she was diagnosed with two medical conditions that prevented her from playing the piano or organ. Unable to teach music at a Presbyterian preschool or play organ on a substitute basis, she simply asked God how she could now best serve Him with the talents He had given her. Three months later, she was stirred to write a poem based on the Parable of the Fig Tree (Luke 13:6-9). She showed this poem to her minister, who asked if she could put it, and any future poems, in the Sunday worship bulletin. Encouraged by the congregation, and particularly Stephanie DeGeneste, Janice has continued to pursue poetry, and at Stephanie's request, Janice has written the preceding poems for each character quality in Chapter 5: Character is the Key. Janice has also served as elder, deacon, Sunday School teacher, and children's choir director at her church, and is a lifelong resident of New Jersey.

Poems By Stephanie M. DeGeneste

a Potpourri:

OH, GLORIOUS KING!

Lord, the work never seems to cease.
Yet through it all, You're my peace.
It's very simple what I must do
Always, only look to You.

You're my hope, my joy, my all in all.
With Your grace, I stand tall.
Your power equips me for anything.
I give my heart to You, oh glorious King.

MY SOUL'S DESIRE

Precious Baby Jesus
Newborn King,
Ultimate Ruler over everything,
I come to You today
In a humble and earnest way
To say
It's my soul's desire
That our hearts be set on fire
With faith, hope, and love
Sent from heaven above.
Newborn King
Ultimate Ruler over everything
I dedicate and commit
My cherished children…Your precious gift
May my life be used for Your glory
As I proclaim the story
Of what You've done for
me
Let them clearly see
And be kindled with Your fire
So it becomes their soul's desire
To seek You while You may be found
So they follow the path to be heaven bound.

WHY THIRST?

Days can be full of fun
When you hop, skip, or run.
Maybe you fall and feel great pain
Or you're stuck indoors staring at the rain.
Whether you're blessed or just feel cursed
Why thirst?

Friends may leave you.
Bullies may scare you
Replacing your smiles with a frown
You want to go up
But people, places, or things pull you down.
When you feel like it's getting worse
Listen to the voice inside that cries,
Why thirst?

Jesus is the Living Water.
Drink 'til you want no more.
No need to wonder what to do
His endless spring of help
Is available to you.
Even when you think your situation is terrible
and it can't get worse
Remember, Jesus is the Living Water
So, Why thirst?

MY GOD, MY GOD

As my feet trod this earthly sod
I cry out, "My God, my God"
I can ill afford
To ignore Your Word.
There must not be a day
That I depart from Your narrow way.

Your Word is a lamp to my feet.
It points the way to Your mercy seat.
How grateful I am
That You are there
To consider my fervent prayers.

So many people and situations
To bring to You.
Only an all-wise God
Knows what to do.

Your ways are best.
My God, please help me
Enter Your rest.
It's so hard to rest
As I trod this sod.
That's why I must cry out,
"My God, my God"

Please help me
To do Your will
I cannot, unless
My soul is still.
Life doles out

Too much each day
That I can't handle
Along the way.

I want to flee.
You tell me stay.
I'll never endure
If I don't obey.

Is life easy?
Oh no, it's hard!
As my feet trod this earthly sod
Lord, hear me as I cry,
"My God. My God."

WHY DOUBT?

Lord, why do I doubt?
What's that about?
When You have so much clout?
Why doubt?

I can't see You
But I know You're there.
Sometimes I can't feel Your love,
But I know You care.

Lord, why do I doubt?
What's that about?
When You have so much clout?
Why doubt?

I've read about people who doubted, too.
What's their excuse?
They walked with You.
Thomas rightly, or maybe wrongly
Earned his name.
Yet, he knew Your frame.
You fulfilled every claim
But all the same
Thomas' lips could also proclaim

Lord, why do I doubt?
What's that about?
When You have so much clout?
Why doubt?

I've heard doubts are foolish
And fears are fruitless,
To be skeptical is rootless.
When I look at the facts
I can only wonder why faith I lack.

You died on Calvary's tree for all, for me.
Up from the grave You arose for all to see.
To allay Thomas' doubt, You appeared to him
So, Your wounds he could touch.
How can any of us doubt
A Savior who loves that much?

Lord, why do I doubt?
What's that about?
When You have so much clout?
Why doubt?

MULLING OVER MIRACLES

When heaven invades earth
So, we can see
Something so superb, so spectacular
Done for others, you or me
That's a miracle!

But why can't we perceive
God working His will and good pleasure
All for His glory and for our good?
Believe...we should!
But we don't, it seems we won't
Recognize the wonderful, notable, or remarkable
Even when they slap us in the face.
We'd rather let Satan and his cohorts erase
The incredible, improbable, exceptional, sublime.
It seems we don't have time
To admire or mull over miracles
Or consider the One who orchestrates them.

We prefer to wade in the waters
Of unbelief and doubt
Refusing to cry out Lord, do MIRACLES today.
Oh venerable One,
Show us Your power in a convincing way.

God, the incredible I AM
Is poised to shatter Satan's shams.
But why won't we let Him?
We refuse to believe or perceive
That which is glorious, fabulous, marvelous
Performed on our behalf so we can receive

His power and so much more.
No, not us, it's the Divine One we deplore
And the Devil's ways we explore

Much to our chagrin
We turn a blind eye and a deaf ear
To MIRACLES that can begin
A life hidden in the secret place of the Most High
Rather than a despondent sigh, we can cry
It's MIRACLES we need now
So we're captivated and wowed
By what God can do.
Yes, we pour out our hopes and dreams to You.
Take up a sacrifice of praise to Your altar.
Lord, help us believe
Your promises are yea and amen.
Grant us faith that unleashes MIRACLES
Again, and again, and again...

THE DAWN OF A NEW DAY

The dawn of a new day
Stirs my soul in a blessed way.
I feast my eyes
On the grandeur of a sunrise.

Oh how majestic is a gorgeous dawn!
It inspires me to go on; To face the day,
Living in His everlasting way
Orange, pink, yellow, and blue
Intermingled in radiant hues.
Dawn's sunrise
Is a veritable feast for my eyes.

I gaze and sigh as I behold the awesome splendor
that only almighty God can render.
Dawn's sounds abound.
God's creatures are heard all around.
Birds sing a paean of praise.
Dogs bark, crickets chime in,
To chant Hallelujah, Amen!

The dawn of a new day,
In its blessed way
Beckons me to begin again
My labor to win the souls of
men.

Appendix C
Resources

www.truewaykids.com	(parent/teacher resources-elementary school children)
www.kidsofintegrity.com	(parent/teacher resources-elementary school children)
www.axis.org	(parent resources for teens)
www.christianbook.com	(miscellaneous items-books, films, music, posters, etc.)
www.motherspray.com	(prayer requests, praise reports, testimonials)
www.lifeway.com	(miscellaneous items)
www.anchordistributors.com	(miscellaneous items)
www.revelationmedia.com	(music, films)
www.iBIBLE App	(animated Bible stories)
www.RightNowMedia.org	(music, films)
www.christianpoets.com	(poetry)
www.christianpoetry.org	(poetry)

www.wordsontheword.com   (poetry)

www.worshiphousemedia.com   (music, films)

www.ccef.org   (Biblical counseling)

www.youtube.com   (worship services, music, liturgical dance, poetry, films)

Appendix D
Discussion Questions

One of the most useful ways to engage with new or even relatively familiar concepts is through discussion, especially with people of diverse perspectives and life experiences. Through conversations with others, one can derive fresh insights, a deeper understanding, and renewed commitment regarding a given topic.

In this section, there are sample discussion questions that can be posed by a facilitator at Blueprint small group sessions.

The primary role of a facilitator is to:

- Be thoroughly familiar with the Discussion Questions prior to the group session
- Ensure needed resources are on hand for the session
- Create a judgment-free space to promote conversation
- Clarify and confirm statements to ensure understanding
- Encourage participation from all members of the group
- Keep the conversation on topic and moving along in a time-efficient way.

The questions that follow should be considered a springboard for discussions.

Suggestions: Rotate facilitators, open and close each session with prayer. In addition to scheduling the discussion, which can occur face-to-face or via video conference, at a convenient time, limit the duration of the session to under two hours.

Introduction

1. What does the New Living Translation of Psalm 127:3, "Children are a gift from the Lord, they are a reward from him," mean to you?

2. Why do you think many parents adopt trendy parenting methods over time-tested Biblical principles?

3. What is one thing you can do differently to build your family's foundation on the rock-solid foundation of God's Word?

4. How can parents who are committed to raising their children in God's way support one another?

Chapter One: The Divine Pattern For The Family

1. Why should God's divine pattern for the family be the jumping-off point for the Christian family?

2. Why is it important to be aware of the varied family configurations that exist today?

3. What kinds of things inform some people's decision to have children without the benefit of marriage?

4. What are some of the factors at play in today's world that make parenting so challenging?

5. There are a number of suggestions provided in Chapter One to increase the probability of a successful marriage: salvation, faithful church attendance, personal Bible study, prayer, regular family devotions and serving the Lord together. Which suggestions have strengthened your marriage? Are there other suggestions that you think are helpful?

Chapter Two: Children Learn What They Live

1. After someone in the group reads Dorothy Nolte's poem aloud, "Children Learn What They Live," discuss which parts of the poem resonate with members of the group.

2. There are seven prerequisites for living a God-centered life in Chapter Two. Ask participants to discuss which ones pose the greatest challenges in their everyday lives. Why?

3. Complete the suggested exercise of listing positive and negative parental influences. Have participants read their list of positives, giving opportunities for the attendees to add to the list.

4. Ask participants to prioritize the most pressing negative influence they'll try to tackle immediately. Provide slips of paper for participants to write down their prioritized negative influence anonymously. After the slips are handed to the facilitator, the negative influences can be read aloud. The facilitator or another group member can pray, asking God to help everyone make progress in their identified areas of need.

5. Exchange ideas on the ways group members can help support one another as they try to cultivate and maintain positive parental influences and whittle away negative parental influences.

Chapter Three: Training The Whole Child

1. After discussing the three aspects (body, soul, spirit) of the child that should be trained, ask which ones the participants find most challenging on a daily basis to incorporate into their children's lives. Why?

2. Seek some suggestions for ways to address the challenges.

3. Talk about the dangers of unregulated screen time.

4. Exchange ideas about easy-to-implement activities that train the three parts of the child.

5. Identify ways parents can support one another as they train the whole child.

Chapter Four: Child-Centered Vs. Christ-Centered Child-Rearing

1. What are your thoughts about having an overarching philosophy that guides your parenting?
2. Discuss the differences between a child-centered and a Christ-centered philosophy.
3. What do you think the greatest disadvantage is of having a child-centered philosophy informing parenting decisions?
4. What are some of the advantages of maintaining a CHRIST-centered philosophy?
5. What parenting styles have you observed firsthand?
6. How can exploring varying parenting styles help or hinder your parenting process?
7. Discuss the implications of the following Scriptures, Jeremiah 29:11 and Isaiah 40:8, on your parenting process.

Chapter Five: Character is the Key

Obedience

1. Discuss the concept of true obedience. Why do you think it's so challenging to obey in this way?
2. What are your thoughts about obedience training for children? What are some of the advantages and disadvantages?
3. How can parents utilize verbal authority to their advantage?
4. What are some of the real-world consequences of not teaching children the importance of obedience?
5. How will looking at and discussing the blessings that come from obedience, as depicted in the Bible, help parents train their children in the way they should go?
6. What are some of the ways parents can reward children for genuine obedience?

7.   How can parents, grandparents, teachers, and other members of the "village" support one another when it comes to teaching children to obey?

Reverence

1.   Discuss the definition of reverence.
2.   Who or what do you reverence?
3.   Disrespect and irreverence are on full display these days; what are some of the most troublesome examples of disrespect that pose negative role modeling for your children?
4.   How can parents foster respect in their homes without being overly heavy-handed?
5.   How can parent-adjacent (peer parents, grandparents, teachers, etc.) adults help support parents as they try to instill respect in their children?

Wisdom

1.   Discuss the differences between godly wisdom and worldly wisdom. Mention the advantages and disadvantages of each type of wisdom.
2.   Proverbs is God's wisdom book. Read the chapter of Proverbs that's associated with the calendar day you're holding the discussion, i.e., on the 10th of the month, you'd read Proverbs 10. Select and discuss verses that relate to any parenting challenges group members are facing.
3.   How can parents develop wisdom networks they can rely on as they seek support when making crucial parenting decisions?

Faith

1. Discuss the Biblical definition of faith as described in Hebrews 11:1.
2. Why do you think child-like faith delights God's heart?
3. What are the areas in your life that you find the hardest to exercise your faith in God?
4. Who or what has helped you become stronger in your faith?
5. How can you help your children walk by faith in ways they can understand?

Honesty

1. Discuss how honesty is presented as a character quality in Chapter Five.
2. It is common today for people to present "alternate facts" and traffic in conspiracy theories. What are some of the implications of dismissing actual facts?
3. What are some of the ways adults demonstrate dishonesty to children?
4. How can children be inspired to be honest in their day-to-day actions?

Patience

1. Discuss the definition of patience.
2. What are some of life's circumstances that cause your patience to wear thin? How do you counteract your impatience in those situations?
3. Cite and discuss some of the impatience-driven actions you've taken and the consequences of those actions.
4. When children observe impatient adults or when adults neglect to teach them to be patient, how does that stunt their emotional and spiritual growth?
5. What are some everyday examples of how you have fostered patience in the lives of your children?

Thankfulness

1. Talk about the meaning of thankfulness. Mention what you think the expression "attitude of gratitude" means.
2. If expressing thankfulness to God for His blessings is important, why do you think so many people have such a difficult time doing so?
3. During the course of a day, what actions can you take to show gratitude to God for His many benefits?
4. Why should children be taught to express gratitude for blessings in tangible ways?
5. Think about people in your family, church community, or social circle who could benefit from an expression of gratitude. What are some of the important things they do that people seldom express appreciation for? What small gratitude gesture can you and/or your child do to show your thankfulness for that person?

Self-Control

1. A working definition of self-control is the ability to do or not do something, even when I want to do something else. In practical terms, what does that mean to you?
2. Cite a few examples of things we know we should do but don't.
3. Cite a few examples of things we shouldn't do but we do.
4. What are some of the ways adult lack of self-control affects children?
5. How can adults support each other to lead more disciplined lives?

Tenderheartedness

1. Discuss the working definition of tenderheartedness and provide examples from the Bible, literature, movies, or current events that depict people demonstrating tenderheartedness.
2. How can parents cultivate tenderheartedness among siblings as the children engage with each other on a regular basis?
3. What kinds of service-based projects can children participate in to develop compassion for others?
4. When family members are together, and they observe someone being unkind or unsympathetic to a person or a pet, how can that situation be used as a "teachable moment?"

Orderliness

1. Orderliness can be described as neatness, having everything in place. Close your eyes for a moment and visualize one room in your house where children engage in multiple types of activities. Would you characterize that room as organized or disorganized? After 3 seconds, say the word aloud that characterizes that room.
2. For those of you who said the room is disorganized, what are some of the contributing factors for that condition?
3. For those of you who said the room is organized, how do you keep it that way?
4. How does organization or disorganization help or hinder the efficiency of your daily routines?
5. What types of activities can the entire family engage in to keep the home environment as organized as possible?

Purity

1. One of the definitions related to purity is careful correctness. When you view your parental role, what does that aspect of purity mean to you?

2. How do you think today's trends related to marriage and the family are impacting children?

3. Given what can be viewed on social media, on TV, in films, and heard in music, how vigilant must parents be to protect their children from harmful influences?

4. How can parents band together to foster safer environments for their children that are free from inappropriate influences?

Forgiveness

1. Read the definition of forgiveness. Sit still for one minute with your eyes closed and see the face of someone you have yet to forgive for some offense committed against you.

2. Sit still for one minute more and envision Jesus on the cross dying for that person's sin and yours as well. Ponder Jesus' words, "Father, forgive them, for they know not what they do."

3. Comment about how that thought experiment made you feel.

4. Biblical forgiveness is vitally important to God. How can we use Jesus' model of forgiveness to inspire us to forgive those who have wronged us?

5. Paul Boese wisely said, "Forgiveness does not change the past, but it does enlarge the future." How might forgiving the person you thought about earlier enlarge the possibilities of your life moving forward?

6. Take a moment to pray for everyone in the group to cultivate forgiveness in their lives.

Chapter Six: Biblical Behavior Modification

Introduction

1. Discuss the concept of biblical behavior modification. What is your greatest takeaway?

2. Of the methods cited in the introduction, which ones are the easiest for you to utilize and which ones are the most difficult? Why?

Prayer

1. What does the verse 1 Thessalonians 5:17, "Pray without ceasing," mean to you?

2. Encourage one or more participants to share one of God's miraculous, unexpected, and/or powerful answers to their prayers.

3. What are some of the challenges associated with praying with your children?

4. What have you done to include your children in times of prayer so that their communication with God is enhanced?

5. How do you handle the times of waiting when it seems like God has not heard your prayers?

6. How do you thank God in word or deed for the answers to your prayers?

7. For those of you who took part in the prayer project, what was the most important take away from completing the exercise?

8. How do you hope to proceed in prayer from this point forward?

Instruction

1. Share your thoughts about being your children's most important teacher throughout their lives.

2. What are the most challenging things to teach your children?

3. Why should helping your child come to saving faith in Jesus Christ be your #1 priority?

4. Why is it so challenging to be diligent when teaching children about spiritual matters?

5. How can adults support each other in this area?

6. Is there a particular Scripture verse that encourages you to be a faithful spiritual guide for your children?

7. Nine teaching methods of Jesus were presented in the Instruction section. Of the nine, which methods appealed to you? Have you tried something new? What were the results?

8. What was your most important takeaway from the Instruction section?

Encouragement

1. Discuss what encouragement entails in the life of children. Why is encouragement so important?

2. Encouragement can take the form of affirmation and rewards. Which forms of encouragement have worked best in your parenting process?

3. In some families, negativity casts a long, dark shadow. How is constant negativity detrimental to children? What can parents do to push positivity?

4. How have you used bonus incentives or rewards, or written notes of encouragement with your children? What were the outcomes?

5. What was your most important takeaway from this discussion or the reading on encouragement?

Correction

1. What is correction and what does God have to say about the importance of correction?
2. Why do you think spanking is frowned upon in our contemporary society?
3. How have your own childhood experiences related to spanking formed your opinion about spanking?
4. What resources have you relied on to guide your perspective on spanking?
5. Discuss the differences between Biblical chastisement and cultural spanking.
6. What discussions have you had with your children about spanking?
7. If you engage in Biblical chastisement, how effective was that method in curbing misbehavior?
8. What food for thought did you receive after reading the Correction section?

Counseling

1. What do the terms counsel and counselor mean to you?
2. One of God's names is Wonderful Counselor. When you ponder the meaning of that name, what thoughts do you have?
3. What are some of the trusted resources that you've used to guide you in your parenting process?
4. Why do you think there's such a stigma attached to seeing a counselor?
5. Why is counseling recommended to help manage life's challenging circumstances?
6. What are the benefits of seeing a Christian counselor?
7. What were some of your important takeaways from the counseling section?

Chapter Seven: Pursue Excellence

1. Discuss the concepts of being intentional and strategic as it pertains to parenting.
2. When you read that parents have a mere 6,574 days until a child turns 18 to make an indelible mark on that child's life, what went through your mind?
3. How beneficial do you think it is to do some sort of formal parent assessment?
4. If both parents are not totally on the same page regarding the need to make parenting improvements, should the committed parent move forward anyway? Why or why not?
5. What are your thoughts about creating a strategic plan for your family?
6. What do you think some of the biggest obstacles will be to executing your plans?
7. How can you overcome those obstacles?
8. What was the most important "Aha" moment that you experienced as you completed *A Blueprint For Building Children: Following God's Plan?*
9. How do you hope God will move in your family on a short-term as well as a long-term basis?

Notes

Below are some of the books, articles, and videos I used in researching this book.

Introduction

1. The American Heritage Dictionary of the English Language, Fifth Edition, 201.

Chapter One: The Divine Pattern For The Family

1. Dictionary.com

Chapter Two: Children Learn What They Live

1. Stormer, John, Growing Up God's Way. Florissant, Missouri, Liberty Bell Press, 1984, 164.
2. goodreads.com/quotes/28871.
3. azquotes.com/author/8211-C-Everett-Koop.
4. Quoted in Our Daily Bread, May 19, 2017.

Chapter Four: Child-Centered Vs. Christ-Centered Child-Rearing

1. Pedersen, James P., The Rise of the Millennial Parents: Parenting Yesterday and Today. Lanham, Maryland, Rowan & Littlefield Education, 2014, 19.
2. "Which Way is the Right Way?" The Parent Test, Created by Charles Wachter, Episode 1, Eureka Productions, 2022.
3. Quoted in Our Daily Bread, April 17, 2015.

Chapter Five: Character is the Key

1. The American Heritage Dictionary of the English Language, Fifth Edition, 311.
2. azquotes.com/author/12558-Jim_Rohn/tag/character.
3. Ibid.
4. azquotes.com/author/19778-Heraclitus.
5. Young, Sarah, Jesus Always: Embracing Joy in His Presence. Nashville, Tennessee, Thomas Nelson, 2016,178.
6. Mason, Babbie. "Trust His Heart." YouTube.Com.
7. Young, Sarah, Jesus Always: Embracing Joy in His Presence. Nashville, Tennessee, Thomas Nelson, 2016, 325.
8. azquotes.com/author/524-Aristotle.
9. Cited in Our Daily Bread, October 22, 2021.
10. quotespedia.org/authors/p/paul-boese/forgiveness-does-not-change-the-past-but-it-does-enlarge-the-future-paul-boese/
11. steelers.com/viseo/jerome-bettis-2015-hall-of-fame-speech-18990528.
12. azquotes.com/author/19778-Heraclitus

Chapter Six: Biblical Behavior Modification

1. Eastman, Dick, The Hour That Changes The World, Grand Rapids, Michigan, Baker Book House, 1983, 11.
2. Ibid,10.
3. The Unger's Bible Dictionary, Third Edition, 992.
4. Dictionary.com
5. goodreads.com/quotes/427508-is-prayer-your-steering-wheel-or-your-spare-tire.
6. Hilgemann, Brandon, "9 Teaching Methods of Jesus," 5 July 2018, propreacher.com/9-teaching- methods-of-jesus/

7. Quote by Dr. Phil on The View, February 26, 2024.

8. azquotes.com/author/5628-Johann_Wolfgang_von_Goethe?p=2.

9. Smith, Brendan L. "The Case Against Spanking." American Psychological Association, Vol. 43, No. 4, 1 April 2012, apa/org/monitor/2012/04/spanking.

10. Dictionary.com

11. Ezzo, Gary and Ann-Marie, Growing Kids God's Way For No Excuse Parenting, Sun Valley, California, 1986, 51.

12. Johnston, David L. "What is Christian Counseling?" YouTube, uploaded by Nothing But the Truth, www.youtube.com/watch?V=bPi7KZDs_bk&t=10s.

Chapter Seven: Pursue Excellence

1. Gilkerson, Luke, and Trisha. "Twelve Self-Assessment Questions for Christian Parents." preachitteachit.org, 7 September 2019, preachitteachit.org/articles/twelve-self-assessment-questions-for-christian-parents/

2. goodreads.com/quotes/851625-what-the-net-seems-to-be-doing-is-chippoing-away.

3. African American Heritage Hymnal, Chicago, Illinois, GIA Publications Inc., 2001, Wash, O God, Our Sons, and Daughters, 674.

Acknowledgments

-I am humbled and honored that my Lord and Savior Jesus Christ placed a call on my life decades ago to do something to help families. Whether as a teacher or principal interacting with parents on a regular basis or as a workshop leader engaging with parents and other concerned adults on a limited basis, I always wanted to offer viable solutions to help children. The Lord enabled me for any and every undertaking because He counted me faithful, putting me into ministry.

-How blessed I am to have had the privilege of parenting two biological children, Aliya and Queintard, II, and one bonus daughter, Kyhara. These three, so precious to me, have emerged as adults that I joyfully look upon with great respect and pride. They helped me in untold ways to strive to be the best parent I could be as they moved through their various stages of growth and development. They have enriched my life in more ways than I will ever be able to convey to them.

-Were it not for grace! Those are the words that embody my feelings when I contemplate the many life challenges that my husband, Queintard, Sr., and I have faced together. God has done great things for us, and I am glad!

-I would be remiss if I did not express appreciation for Mario and Erika Williams. From the first time they went through the "A Blueprint For Building Children: Following God's Plan" workshop, they caught the vision that God's way of raising and educating children is the better way. They constantly encouraged me in my endeavors and persistently prodded me to expand my work to *have a greater outreach to parents seeking better ways to train their children in the way they should go.*

-How can I say thanks to my "real" editor, Karen Renzo? As songwriter Andre Crouch stated, "The voices of a million angels could not express my gratitude." My heart overflows with appreciation for someone who has believed in and supported Blueprint from its inception. She prayed for the work in its many iterations and always provided constructive feedback and the encouragement I needed to persevere. Our decades-long friendship and faith-filled fellowship have produced a bounty of good fruit. How blessed we are that we can taste and see that the Lord is good!

-To everyone who participated in the Correction section focus group or one-on-one phone interviews, I thank you for the privilege and pleasure of your time. Your insights certainly gave me food for thought, and I believe the inclusion of your observations gleaned from my conversations with you will be very beneficial to Blueprint's readers as well.

-To Kyle Adams, the cover artist, I express my gratitude for taking on the project while navigating the ever-increasing number of important and exciting opportunities that keep coming your way. From the time you entered New Covenant Christian Academy in its inaugural year as a kindergartener, I knew God had His hand on your life, and He would use you in mighty ways. Never, ever could I have imagined that the Lord would bless me in such a special and profound way by using your gifted hands to create original cover art for my book.

-To Janice Haer, a precious sister in the faith and "poet extraordinaire," I thank you for writing the Character is the Key poems. Your creative expression and life of dedicated service to the people of God, especially His wee little ones, are things I greatly admire. You had to persevere through some difficult, demanding, and, at times, disheartening days to complete your contribution. I believe your work will be a blessing to the readers of A Blueprint For Building Children: Following God's Plan.

-With time being the most precious commodity any of us has to steward wisely, I truly thank Erika, Nadine, and Sarah, who accepted my invitation and were able to read through Blueprint, despite their incredibly demanding schedules, and make remarks for subsequent readers to consider. Each one of you brings a unique perspective to the table, but most important to me, each one of you lives a life worthy of the call God has placed upon it.

To Rachel, Sheldon, and your teams, I thank you for your integrity and the wonderful work needed to rescue the Blueprint project from the debacle that threatened to derail it. There is no doubt in my mind that in God's sovereignty, He brought us together for such a time as this.

-To the readers of A Blueprint For Building Children: Following God's Plan, I want you to know that I'll continue to pray for you. It is the deepest desire of my heart that something in this book ignites the fire of change in your life. I hope you'll let the ultimate Change Agent guide you to make ongoing modifications to perfect your parenting process. My prayer is that by grace and truth, you will live the type of life that builds up your children and the children in your sphere of influence into godly men and women who'll make a difference in this world for the glory of God.

About the Author

STEPHANIE M. DEGENESTE is a champion for the cause of building stronger families. As a career educator for over fifty years, Stephanie has seen how the power of family and "village" influences can deeply impact children. She is the author of *What God Can Do With a Slice of Bread and a Teaspoon of Peanut Butter*, a memoir about the miraculous inception of the Christian school she and her husband established in 2006. Stephanie holds a Master of Science degree in Education and has been certified in Biblical Counseling Studies from the Christian Counseling & Educational Foundation. She has served in both secular and Christian environments as an educational leader, working with entry-level employees to CEOs and students of all ages, parents, faculty, and community stakeholders in the academic arena. Stephanie and her husband are blessed with three adult children and two grandchildren. They currently live in North Carolina.

Connect Online

Website: www.wgcdproductions.com
Email: stephanie@wgcdproductions.com
IG: @stephaniedegeneste